mply to know the
nd thought in the
turn making that
rrent of true and

of Criticism At
365.

VENETIA
CITTÀ NOBILISS.ᵃ E SINGOLARE
DESCRITTA DAL SANSOVINO CON NOVE E COPIO
AGGIVNTE DI D. GIVSTINIAN MARTINIONI.

'Venetia'. Title-page of a guide to Venice 1662

Milton Grundy
VENICE
An Anthology Guide

Preface by John Julius Norwich

A & C Black
London

First published, 1971,
by Anthony Blond Ltd, London
Second edition, 1976, and third revised
edition, 1980, published by Lund
Humphries Publishers Ltd, London

Fourth, revised edition, 1985, in new
format, in paperback

Published by A & C Black (Publishers)
Limited
35 Bedford Row
London WC1R 4JH

ISBN 0 7136 2780 8

Created for the Publishers by
Lund Humphries Publishers Ltd
Typeset by Keyspools Ltd, Golborne,
Warrington
Made and printed in Great Britain by
Camelot Press, Southampton

Contents

Acknowledgments

The author wishes to thank the following publishers and individuals who have kindly granted permission to quote throughout this anthology, and to illustrate the walks:

Allen & Unwin: *Venice* by A. J. C. Hare and St Clair Baddeley, *Modern Painters* and *The Stones of Venice* by John Ruskin.
The Athlone Press: *A History of Architecture on the Comparative Method* by Sir Banister Fletcher.
Batsford: *The Architectural History of Venice* by D. Howard
Cassell: *La Serenissima* by A. Lowe.
Clarendon Press: *The Italian Painters of the Renaissance* by B. Berenson.
Collins: *Italian Journey* by J. W. von Goethe, *The Companion guide to Venice* by Hugh Honour.
The Dumbarton Oaks Research Library and Collection, Trustees for Harvard University: *The Church of San Marco in Venice* by O. Demus.
Elek Books: *Venice, The Masque of Italy* by M. Brion.
Faber & Faber: *Venice* by J. Morris.
Gentry Books: *Gondola, Gondolier* by T. Holme.
Hamish Hamilton: *No Magic Eden* by S. Guiton.
Istituto Poligrafico dello Stato: *Venice and its Lagoons* by G. Lorenzetti.
Macdonald: *Italian Food* by E. David.
Methuen: *Permanent Red* by J. Berger and *A Wanderer in Venice* by E. V. Lucas.
Muller: *Renaissance Architecture in Venice* by R. Lieberman
L'Œil: 'Venice Observed' (notes on the plates) by A. Chastel.
Parrish: *The Lagoon of Venice* by S. Sprigge.
Oxford University Press: *Giovanni Bellini* by G. Robertson.
Penguin Books: *An Outline of European Architecture* by Sir Nikolaus Pevsner and *Art and architecture in Italy* by R. Wittkower.
Phaidon: *The Civilisation of the Renaissance in Italy* by J. Burckhardt, *The Story of Art* by E. H. Gombrich, *An Introduction to Italian Renaissance Painting* by C. Gould and *Painting in XVIII Century Venice* by M. Levey.
Princeton University Press: *A Renaissance of Early Christian Art in 13 Century Venice* and *Late Classical and Mediaeval Studies in honour of Albert Matthias Friend Jr.* (ed. K. Weistman) by O. Demus.
Skira: *The Venice of Carpaccio* by T. Pignatti.
Thames & Hudson: *Venice* by H. Decker, *Italian villas and palaces* by G. Masson, *A concise history of Venetian painting* by J. Steer and *Venetian Art from Bellini to Titian* by J. Wilde.
Weidenfeld & Nicolson: *Venice: A Thousand Years of Culture and Civilization* by P. Lauritzen.
Yale: *Paintings in Cinquecento Venice* by D. Rosand

The Canaletto painting on the cover is reproduced by gracious permission of H.M. The Queen. The following drawings and etchings are reproduced by courtesy of the Giorgio Cini Foundation (page 153), the Correr Museum (page 25), the Goethe-Schiller-Archives, Weimar (page 53). All other drawings and etchings are reproduced by courtesy of the Trustees of the British Museum, Prints and Drawings Department. The line drawings are by Kaffe Fasset.

List of illustrations

Preface

On 14 July 1902, at eight minutes to ten in the morning, the great campanile that had stood for almost a thousand years at the corner of St Mark's Square in Vencie shuddered, shook itself, split open and collapsed in a pile of rubble. There was only one casualty: the custodian's cat. Otherwise, not a soul was hurt, not a stone displaced from the great basilica or the Doges' Palace. '*Il Campanile*,' said the Venetians, '*è stato galantuomo*' – 'the campanile has behaved like a gentleman.' Almost immediately the rebuilding began; and on 25 April 1912, a millennium to the day after the foundation of its predecessor, the present virtually identical tower was inaugurated.

That story thus has a happy ending. The disaster befell a single edifice and, what was luckier still, the one great monument in all Venice that could – more or less – be replaced. But the fall of the campanile proved a warning of worse to come; for now it is the whole city that is in peril. The sea, on which it has relied for fifteen centuries for its protection and preservation – that same Adriatic which the Doges used ceremonially to wed with a golden ring – now threatens to engulf it; and if the world does not at once come to its rescue, then, in roughly the same period that has elapsed since the campanile fell – within the lifetime of many children alive today – Venice as we know it will have ceased to exist.

This, let me emphasize, is not just a piece of hysterical alarmism; it is cold, scientific fact. The lagoon in which Venice stands measures some 300 square miles, yet much of it is only two or three feet deep. Protected from the open sea by a thin tongue of low-lying land to the east, it remains linked to it by three narrow gaps through which the tide flows in and out twice a day, incidentally providing the city with its only system of drainage. There can be few other places in the world where the balance of land and water is so precariously maintained; and when it is upset, Venice is flooded.

Now these floods are no new phenomenon in themselves; we have all seen countless photographs of gondolas crossing the middle of the Piazza or people being carried piggy-back across it. What is sinister is that they are becoming more and more frequent; over the past twenty years there have been well over forty floods of three and a half feet or higher – more than in the previous century. And in the worst disaster of recent years, that of 4 November 1966, the waters reached a height of 6 ft 4 in. above normal and remained there for nearly twenty-four remorseless hours.

The surprising thing about this particular flood was that it owed practically nothing to rainfall or even to tide. It was the effect, almost entirely, of the wind. For two days already there had been a strong north-easterly gale, piling up the seas along the Adriatic coast. Then, on the morning of the 4th, it veered round to the south-east – the axis of the Adriatic, which is, if you come to think of it, a long cul-de-sac – and at the same time increased in force, driving the accumulated water into the Lagoon, not only through the three channels but even over the *murazzi*, the old sea walls with which the Doges had strengthened the outer rim. Fortunately it was a season of neap tides, when the gravitational forces of the sun and the moon pull in opposing directions so that the tidal effect is minimized. Had there, on the other hand, been a spring tide – which could equally well have been the case – Venice would have been submerged under nine or ten feet of muddy, oily water, with results that one would rather not contemplate.

But, it may be objected, the weather is surely no worse than it used to be; why then is Venice now being flooded more and more often, two or three times a year? The answer is simple and sad: she is growing ever more vulnerable, so that she must now surrender to assaults which in former days she would have taken in her stride. For the whole bed of the Lagoon is subsiding, in some districts at the terrifying rate of an inch every ten years. And those districts, alas, include the Piazza and St Mark's itself – the soggiest and most unstable part of the whole city. During the same period, the level of the sea is rising by about half an inch, owing to the gradual melting of polar ice and other phenomena too technical for us laymen to understand.

Now there is obviously little we can do about polar ice; but subsidence is a different matter, since this is largely due to the huge industrial complexes which continue to proliferate along the landward side of the Lagoon. When the industrial zone around Mestre and Marghere was first planned, its object was admirable – to provide employment for the Venetians and to give a much-needed boost to their economy without desecrating the city itself. Unfortunately, heavy industries are apt to need enormous quantities of fresh water; and instead of piping this down from the mountains, the designers of the new plant preferred to drive wells indiscriminately into the water-table that underlies the Lagoon. As a result, the bed of the Lagoon has subsided, and Venice with it.

The third prong of the attack is perhaps the most insidious of all since, unlike the others, it is a constant. The Venetian air, moist and heavily saline, has always tended to corrode the stones of the city; in recent years, however, it has become charged with sulphurous fumes from the industrial areas – and, to a lesser degree, from the oil-fired heating systems in Venice itself; and the combination of these fumes with the humidity and the salinity produces a hideously corrosive atmosphere which is, quite simply, eating away the materials – not only the stone, but also the marble and brick, even the bronze – of which the city is made.

Such, then, is the three-fold menace; what is being done? Surprisingly, perhaps, the danger from the sea should prove relatively easy to control, by the construction of lock gates which will be able to close off one or more of the three entrances to the lagoon whenever the high waters threaten. Preliminary work on these has already begun. The whole system could be completed in very few years, after which Venice will be safer from the sea than at any time in her history. As for subsidence, the sinking of any new wells has already been prohibited by law, and two aqueducts have now been completed which provide the industrial zones and Venice itself with all the fresh water they need. Thus, though St Mark's itself still gives cause for concern, the general threat to the city is mercifully diminishing. The probelm of atmospheric pollution is a good deal harder to solve, but, here too, much progress has already been made: increasingly severe controls are being imposed on industries and residents alike – all Venetian domestic heating has now been converted from heavy fuel oil to methane gas – and the regular monitoring reports show that the air in the city, though still not as clean as it should be, is at least improving steadily.

But the fact remains that progress is still nowhere near as fast as it should be; and meanwhile the slow, silent devastation goes on. In an effort to combat this, and recognizing that the problem of Venice is far too large for any one country to tackle single-handed, some two dozen private organizations (of which Venice in Peril is one) from almost as many foreign countries are at work raising money and themselves restoring such monuments, large and small, as might well otherwise crumble away. They work in close collaboration with the Venetian authorities as well as with UNESCO, which has a permanent office in the Piazza San Marco; and thanks to them some sixty projects have already been completed or are well on the way. They include the Salute and Santi Giovanni e Paolo, San Zaccaria and Santa Maria dei Miracoli, the Veroneses at San Sebastiano, the Tiepolos at the Carmini and the Tintorettos at San Rocco. British funds were responsible for the restoration of the Madonna dell'Orto, Sansovino's Loggetta at the base of the campanile of St Mark, San Nicolò dei Mendicoli, the Porta della

Carta, the stained glass of SS. Giovanni e Paolo and the mosaics at
Torcello. Our latest restoration, undertaken in collaboration with our
Dutch, Swedish and Texan colleagues, is that of the exquisite little
Oratorio dei Crociferi, just opposite the church of the Gesuiti.

The International Fund for Monuments Inc, an organization with
headquarters in the United States, has also played a distinguished role in
the restoration of the Venetian monuments. They have restored the
church of Santa Maria del Giglio (the 'Zobenigo'), the church of the Pietà,
and the great cycle of thirty-eight canvases painted by Tintoretto for the
Scuola Grande di San Rocco.

All these projects are acts of faith – faith in Venice's future – born of a
determination that the most beautiful city in the world and the one
which, for its size, has made a greater contribution to our civilization
than any other, shall not be allowed to perish. Her salvation will be
expensive – indeed, prohibitive if thought of in national terms. But
Venice, surely, belongs not just to Italy but to the world, and once the
task is seen as a world responsibility it becomes a perfectly manageable
proposition. Venice *can* be saved, and will be – if her friends do no betray
her. If they turn away now, she will fall; softly, slowly, silently, but every
bit as surely as the campanile did, that July morning eighty-three years
ago.

JOHN JULIUS NORWICH   1985

If you have bought this book you have already made a contribution to Venice in
Peril (VIP) and to the International Fund for Monuments (IFM) who receive the
author's royalties on each copy. But these organizations continue to need
support, and look to people like you, Dear Reader, for it. The International Fund
for Monuments issues a membership card, which entitles the holder to free
admission to museums and galleries and to discounts in hotels, restaurants and
shops: details can be obtained from the Fund's Venice office at the Scuola Grande
di San Giovanni Evangelista (see p.148) – MG.

Introduction

This is a new edition of my *anthology guide* of 1980. Like its predecessor, it is essentially an anthology arranged as a guide book. It is a common experience that the information for the tourist (both in books and by human guides) falls miserably short of the best that has been thought and said on the subject. In Venice I find this particularly galling, for it is a significant part of the experience of the place that other and far more distinguished visitors have been before and pondered upon the very sight that is before one's eyes. I have therefore chosen what seem to me to be the most illuminating passages from their writings, and arranged these in the context of tours of the town. Something of this kind was done by Augustus Hare at the turn of the century. But I have looked in vain for a modern equivalent, and (not for the first time in my life) I find I have had to write the book I wanted to read. In doing this I have had to make a number of basic decisions, and perhaps at this stage I should say what they are.

In the first place, I have concentrated on passages which illuminate particular pictures, buildings or views. I have omitted passages which throw light only on their author (though with Ruskin I have made some exceptions, for he is such a towering phenomenon that I expect the reader may be interested in him in his own right).

You will notice, too, that I do not expect the reader to see everything. If you are in Venice for three months you will be able to make use of *Venice* by Giulio Lorenzetti – a thorough and scholarly work (to which I have referred ceaselessly in preparing this book). In a stay of two weeks (or in the first two weeks of a longer stay) it is plainly better to take an informed look at a relatively small number of masterpieces, than to tramp in an uninformed way past a bewildering number of objects of diverse styles, periods and quality. I have therefore had to make a lot of decisions about what to include and what to omit. I have not found it necessary to depart in any radical way from currently accepted notions of what are masterpieces, but I have made a conscious effort not to be influenced by famous names, and I have not hesitated to omit things which do not live up to their reputations. I have also (though with some reluctance) left out a few things simply on the grounds that they are too far away from the seven areas into which I have divided the town: those of major importance are mentioned in the Appendices.

This version of the book follows the general pattern of earlier editions, almost all the quotations from the 1980 edition have been retained and a number of new ones added. What is fundamentally new about this version of the book is that it directs the reader's attention to the restorations which have been carried out – mainly during the past few years – as part of the international campaign to rescue the city from decay. I need say nothing here about the importance of that campaign: Lord Norwich in his preface gives an account of its aims and progress. But the restorations themselves deserve specific mention, and I draw attention to all the more significant achievements of the restorers, as each of the monuments occurs in the text. Not all the restoration work leaves any visible result, but where it does – e.g. on the Loggetta in the Piazza – the effect can be quite stunning, and for that reason alone any modern guide book should, I think, make a point of directing the reader to what is now a fascinating series of new experiences.

The city calls for a variety of responses – the earnestness of Ruskin can be felt as inappropriate at some times, as can the 'amused' stance of Morris at others. The one response which – as the reader will inevitably discover for himself – is unproductive at all times is art-indigestion, and I should perhaps stress – especially for the more serious-minded visitor – that there is such a thing as an experience of the town as a whole, which is not obtained by scurrying (with however informed a sensibility) from one picture or building to another. You will see that I propose only seven principal excursions: I suggest that not every morning be devoted to sightseeing, but that a lot of one's time in Venice ought to be devoted to doing nothing in particular – strolling in the Piazza, taking morning coffee in some campo, or just getting lost in the maze of small alleyways.

No doubt the best way to approach Venice is from the sea; but the visitor arriving by air can get something of the effect if he takes the motor launch from the airport across the Lagoon.

I intend that all the principal excursions be done in the morning: museums, churches and galleries are open, and the sunshine helps one to see the pictures. The best way to do these excursions in the summertime is to start not later than eight in the morning (earlier if possible); you can then take them at a leisurely pace, have time for sitting down, and for coffee, and still escape the hottest part of the day. If the day is sunny and hot, you can reckon to be on the boat going over to the Lido before noon. I think bathers will want to do the other afternoon excursions on days which are too windy or too cloudy for the Lido, but these excursions are not energetic ones and can be done on the hottest afternoons.

I do not expect that the reader will necessarily do a whole walk in a single morning. I indicate in Walks 2 and 3 a possible dividing point, but I should like the reader to approach every walk with the resolve to give up at the point where visual indigestion or weary feet require. Sunday is not a good day for any of the walks: it is annoying to find that a church service prevents one from seeing the painting one most wishes to see. For a Sunday, the reader may pick out the Correr from Walk 1, the Accademia or the Peggy Guggenheim Collection (which, like the Correr has the great merit of being open in the afternoon) from Walk 2, the Scuola degli Schiavoni from Walk 3, the Querini-Stampalia from Walk 4, the Scuola di San Rocco, the Scuola dei Carmini or the Ca'Rezzonico from Walk 5, the Ca'd'Oro from Walk 6, or some of the Special Interests from Appendix 2.

The Tourist Office, under the arcade at the far end of the Piazza, will provide you with a useful map and information on current events. Ascertain opening times (and *days*) of collections you plan to see. At the time of writing, the Correr (Walk 1) is closed on Tuesdays, the Accademia and the Guggenheim (Walk 2) on Mondays and Tuesdays respectively, San Giorgio degli Schiavoni and the Greek Institute (Walk 3) on Mondays and Tuesdays respectively and the Querini-Stampalia (Walk 4) on Mondays; in Walk 5, San Giovanni Evangelista is closed on Saturdays and Sundays, the Scuola dei Carmini on Sundays, and the Ca'Rezzonico on Fridays, and in Walk 6, the Ca'd'Oro is closed on Mondays. Staff problems cause museums to close some rooms from time to time; if you are concerned to see a particular item ascertain from the ticket office whether the room is open. One last practical tip: if you have to find a building by its street and number, remember that Venetian numbering continues throughout a district without regard to changes of street.

Confusingly, though charmingly, the street signs are in Venetian dialect: I have used the Italian versions of place names, except where the directions involve the reader in consulting the street signs.

Once again I am indebted to many friends for suggestions and improvements and for acting as guinea-pigs; it is very difficult to tell how a book of this kind is going to work in practice, and I should be grateful to readers for any proposals for improving another edition. I should like to acknowledge the help and encouragement of V. I. Atroshenko and Andrew Williams; I am particularly indebted to Lord Norwich for his preface, and to Philip Rylands for a great deal of information about the progress of various restorations (or lack of it), much of which has been embodied into the text without further acknowledgement.

MILTON GRUNDY   London **1985**

Streets full of water. Please advise.
ROBERT BENCHLEY

Walk I

San Giorgio – San Marco – Piazza – Ducal Palace – Correr Museum

San Giorgio Maggiore

This walk begins with a general view of the city from the top of the bell-tower of San Giorgio. From the Piazza, walk towards the water, turn left and continue over two bridges. Take the vaporetto (line 5 or 8) to San Giorgio.

The late c16 church of San Giorgio Maggiore (summer opening times 9–12.30; 14.00–19.00) is one of Palladio's most distinguished works. Follow the arrows to the campanile: from the belfry is a fine view of the city, the lagoon and the mainland. Sea-going vessels sail through the Lagoon, but much of it is shallow and treacherous, and one can easily imagine how its muddy flats and islands provided a refuge for inhabitants of the Roman towns on the mainland fleeing before the barbarian invasions in the c5 and c6. Venice's economic success came from its sea-trade and sea-power; the Venetians dominated the trade between Europe and the East from the c9 until Vasco da Gama circumnavigated Africa at the end of the c15, and the vast wealth accumulated during that period saw them through three centuries of economic decline in (as the buildings all around us testify) unparalleled style.

Down below us, on the south side, can be seen the former monastery buildings which now house the Cini Foundation: the courtyard to the left is c16, that on the right is by Longhena, c17.

We return to the church; there is a door into the chancel.   .

From any point in the church one is aware of the presence of the focus of the composition. This is the single great dome over the crossing, placed exactly midway between the entrance and the high altar, and brightly lit by windows in the lantern and drum. The four barrel-vaulted spaces which meet at this point – in the nave, the two transepts and the chancel – are clearly differentiated from the side aisles, which are lower and cross-vaulted, in order to draw attention to the four arms of the cross. In this way Palladio deftly combined his classical preference for centrally planned temples with the Christian ideal of the cruciform plan.

The giant Composite order of half columns and piers and the smaller order of Corinthian pilasters are both carried consistently around the whole church, as well

as being echoed on the façade. The smaller order orientates the spectator walking
round the church, helping him to relate himself to the huge space. At the same
time the giant order, raised on high bases and stressed by a boldly dentilled
cornice, serves to articulate more distant vistas.

Great thermal windows admit light to the nave, side aisles and chancel. The
thermal window, a lunette divided vertically into three sections, is so-called
because of its derivation from Roman baths or *thermae*. The baths were a major
source of inspiration for Palladio, not only providing him with individual motifs
but also suggesting ways in which spaces of different shapes and sizes could be
organized coherently. At this stage the thermal window was still rarely used in
Italian architecture, but after Palladio demonstrated its possibilities it became
very popular in Venice. From this time on thermal windows became standard
features of new churches, and were also inserted into many older ones to improve
the lighting.

HOWARD

On the walls of the chancel are two pictures, best seen from the altar rail.
On the left wall
Tintoretto: *The Fall of Manna*

One of Tintoret's most remarkable landscapes. Another painter would have
made the congregation hurrying to gather [the Manna] and wondering at it.
Tintoret at once makes us remember that they have been fed with it 'by space
of forty years.'

RUSKIN

On the right wall
Tintoretto: *The Last Supper*.

It was the whole scene that Tintoret seemed to have beheld in a flash of
inspiration intense enough to stamp it ineffaceably on his perception: and it was
the whole scene, complete, peculiar, individual, unprecedented, that he
committed to canvas with all the vehemence of his talent. Compare his 'Last
Supper' at San Giorgio – its long, diagonally placed table, its dusky spaciousness,
its scattered lamp-light and halo-light, its startled gesticulating figures, its
richly realistic foreground – with the customary formal, almost mathematical
rendering of the subject, in which impressiveness seems to have been sought in
elimination rather than comprehension. You get from Tintoret's work the
impression that he felt, pictorially, the great, beautiful, terrible spectacle of
human life very much as Shakespeare felt it poetically — with a heart that never
ceased to beat a passionate accompaniment to every stroke of his brush.

HENRY JAMES

In the Last Supper of S. Giorgio, one of his latest works, the extent of
Tintoretto's deviation from Renaissance precepts may be readily measured by
comparing it with the classic example of that time – Leonardo's. In Tintoretto's
picture the viewpoint is very high – we are looking down on the room from above
the heads of the figures – and the recession of the table is odd and irrational in
its violent asymmetry in the picture space. Of the individual figures it may be

In 1720 Domenico Lovisa published a two-volume collection of engravings by various artists with the title 'Gran Teatro delle Più Insigni Prospettive a Venezia' ('Gran Teatro di Venezia'). Fillipo Vasconi (1687–1730) was the editor and a prominent contributor.

noted that the servant in the right foreground, seen from the back balanced on one foot and making an affected gesture with his left hand while turning to the kneeling woman, would not be out of place in any Central Italian Mannerist composition. He in fact constitutes the main formal balance to the violent perspective of the table. But we only notice him late, if at all; (both here and in the Agony[1] the faces of nearly all the figures are either averted or in shadow: this principle is fundamental to Tintoretto's art). Our eyes are directed to Christ with His own mysterious light, to the fiercely burning lamp (perhaps symbolizing the Holy Spirit) and to the ghostly cherubim who sweep down through the ceiling.

GOULD

The c16 choir stalls show scenes from the life of Saint Benedict. On the left is the entrance to the Sacristy (across passage), with c17 panelling and an attractive clock on the wall.

We leave the church by the w door, take the vaporetto back to the San Zaccaria stop on the Riva degli Schiavoni ('of the slavs'), and return to the Piazza, to visit the Basilica of San Marco (open 9.30–17.30).

---

[1] In the Scuola di San Rocco, p.137.

San Marco

Enter the central portal and take the stairs to the upper galleries (open 10.00–18.00), emerge on the balcony beside the horses, and go to the left-hand corner where a porphyry head sticks up from the balustrade. This is c8 Syrian, believed to represent the Byzantine emperor 'of the broken nose', Justinian II. Just around the corner and on the wall on the left is a Byzantine style madonna, probably c13, with votive lamps on either side. This, says Hare,

> . . . commemorates the remorse of the Council of Ten for the unjust condemnation of Giovanni Grassi (1611), pardoned ten years after his execution. He swore that the senators who condemned him would all die within the year, and they all obliged him. The lamps were lighted afterwards whenever an execution took place, and the condemned, before mounting the scaffold, turned round to the picture, and repeated the '*Salve Regina*'. The popular tradition of Venice asserts that the two little lamps which constantly burn on this, the south-west side of the church, commemorate the 'Morte Innocente' or *buon anima del fornaretto*, of a baker's boy who (1507) was tried, condemned, and executed for murder – though innocent – because he had picked up the sheath of a dagger with which a murder had been committed in a neighbouring calle, and it had been found in his possession.

Lorenzetti says the lamps were left as a thank-offering by a sailor saved from a storm.

Looking over the edge of the balustrade, you can see the two square pillars of Acre. Believed to be Syrian c5, they are part of the loot brought to Venice from wars in the Near East.

If you look out towards the Lagoon and the island of San Giorgio, with Palladio's church on it, you will see on the left part of the arcaded façade of the Ducal Palace, on the right Sansovino's Library, and, between, the Piazzetta. Just this side of the Ducal Palace is a large gateway – the Porta della Carta, and at the foot of that (on the left) a group of porphyry figures, Egyptian c4, representing Diocletian and Constantius and their heirs, the emperors of the western and eastern Roman empires. From the ground you can see holes in the helmets where royal crowns were formerly fixed. They are popularly called 'The Moors'.

The pavement mosaics around the high altar in San Marco. A detail of an illustration from the book of plates by Giovanni and Luigi Kreutz, published in 1843 in a special edition for presentation to the Austrian Emperor Ferdinand on the occasion of his visit.

A group of porphyry figures.

These notable brothers came from Albania together in a ship laden with great
store of riches. After their arrival in Venice which was the place whereunto they
were bound, two of them went on shore and left the other two in the ship. They
two that were landed entered into a consultation and conspiracy how they might
dispatch their other brothers which remained in the ship, to the end they might
gaine all the riches to themselues. Whereupon they bought themselues some
drugges to that purpose, and determined at a banquet to present the same to
their other brothers in a potion or otherwise. Likewise on the other side those two
brothers that were left in the shippe whispered secretly amongst themselues
how they might make away with their brothers that were landed, that they
might get all the wealth to themselues. And thereupon procured means
accordingly. At last this was the final issue of those consultations. They that had
beene at land presented to their other brothers certaine poysoned drugges at a
banquet to the end to kill them, which those brothers did eat and dyed therewith,
but not incontinently. For before they ministered a certain poysoned march-
pane or some other such thing at the uery same banquet to their brothers that
had been at land; both with poysons when they had thoroughly wrought their
effects upon both couples, all four dyed shortly after. Whereupon the Signiory of
Venice seized upon all their goods as their own, which was the first treasure that
euer Venice possessed, and the first occasion of inriching the estate; and in
memoriall of that uncharitable and unbrotherly conspiracy, hath erected the
pourtraitures of them in porphyrie as I said before in two seuerall couples
consulting together.
CORYAT

The two columns at the end of the Piazzetta each carry a statue – one of a lion and one of Saint Theodore.

. . . S. Theodore (San Todero) martir et cavalier di Dio – standing on a crocodile
(by *Pietro Guilombardo* 1329) – the Byzantine saint who was patron of the
Republic before the body of S. Mark was brought from Egypt in 827. Doge
Sebastino Ziani (1172–78), having promised any 'onesta grazia' to the man who
should safely lift the columns to their places, it was claimed by Nicolo il
Barattiere, who demanded that he should be permitted to establish public
gambling tables between these pillars. The promise could not be revoked; but
to render it of no effect, public executions (previously carried out near San
Giovanni in Bragora), were also ordained to be done here so as to make it a place
of ill-omen.
HARE

On the one nearest to the Ducal Palace stands the lion of St. Mark in bronze
once *fulgente d'oro* (shining with gold). Originally it was probably a 'chimera'
and it has been much discussed, having been considered to be Etruscan by some
or Persian of the Sassanid period (IV cent. B.C.) or, according to more recent
attributions, a Chinese *'chimera'* the wings having been added to make it a
symbol of St. Mark. It was carried off to Paris by the French in 1797 and brought
back in 1815 in so bad a state as to require to be partly recast. On the top of the
column towards the Library is the marble figure of San Todero (St. Theodore) the
Greek saint who was the first patron saint of the Veneto people. The statue is
made up of various pieces: the head is of Parian marble, and, according to the

most recent studies and comparisons, must be a fine *portrait of Mithridates King of Pontus*; the torso is Roman art of the period of Hadrian with the missing parts added; these latter and the *dragon*, by comparing them with the sculpture on the crowning of St. Mark's show traces of Lombardic art of the first half of the XV cent. The statue actually on the column, on a modern base (dated) is an exact copy of the original which is now kept in the Ducal Palace owing to its very bad state of preservation.
LORENZETTI

Sansovino, Florentine sculptor and architect, fled the sack of Rome in **1527** and settled in Venice. His grasp of the economics of property development strikes a modern note.

In the year 1529 there were butchers' stalls between the two columns of the Piazza, with a number of small wooden booths, used for the vilest purposes, and a shame as well as deformity to the place, offending the dignity of the Palace and the Piazza, while they could not but disgust all strangers who made their entry into Venice, by the side of San Giorgio.

Sansovino caused these booths and stalls to be removed; he then erected the butchers' shops where they are now, and, adding to these certain stalls for the dealers in vegetables, he increased the revenues of the Procuranzia by seven hundred ducats yearly, while he beautified the Piazza and the city by the same act. No long time afterwards, he observed that by removing one house in the Merceria (near the clock, and on the way to the Rialto), which paid a rent of twenty-six ducats only, he could open a street into the Spadaria by which the value of the houses and shops all around would be much increased; he took down that house accordingly, thereby adding a hundred and fifty ducats to the income of the Procuranzia. He built the Hostelry of the Pellegrino, moreover, on the same site with another on the Campo Rusulo; and these together brought in four hundred ducats. His buildings in the Pescaria and other parts of the city, houses as well as shops, and erected at various times, were also of the utmost utility, and altogether the Procuranzia gained by means of Sansovino, an addition of no less than two thousand ducats per annum, so that they might well hold him in esteem.
VASARI

Sansovino's Library (Libreria Sansoviniana) is perhaps one of the most monumental works in Venice. Yet, as Decker puts it, 'Venetian buildings retain, above all, anthropomorphous dimensions; they are never monumental in the sense that ancient Roman art, conceived by the Latin

---

From 1741 until about 1744 Canaletto drew and etched a number of Venetian scenes. These views have a vitality and freshness not found in engravings done from his work by other printers. Right, the bird-market scene on the Molo between the two columns shows, in the background, the striped-awning covered barge where convicted prisoners were kept until deportation. The view (below) of the Prison looks down the Riva degli Schiavoni.

spirit, was monumental.' Motifs from the façade occur in many later
buildings – the Ca' Rezzonico, for example (see p.135).

The small building at the foot of the Campanile – the Loggetta – was
also designed by Sansovino. His also are the four bronze statues in the
niches, though the terrace and balustrade are a c17 and the bronze gate
an c18 addition.

> The draperies by his hand are, indeed, most delicately beautiful; finely folded,
> they preserve to perfection the distinction between the nude and draped portions
> of the form. His children are soft, flexible figures, with none of the muscular
> development proper only to adults; the little round legs and arms are truly of
> flesh, and in no wise different to those of Nature herself. The faces of his women
> are sweet and lovely.
> VASARI

All were demolished when the Campanile fell on 14 July 1902, and
reassembled (with new marble facings to the end walls) in 1912 when the
Campanile was rebuilt. The reliefs, the bronze statues and the great
variety of different marbles used in it have all been beautifully restored
by the British Venice in Peril Fund. The Fund has recently completed a
similarly comprehensive restoration of the Porta della Carta (which we
shall see at closer quarters later – see p.48).

Piazza

We turn now to the Piazza. Down the right side runs the Procuratie
Vecchie (c16) and down the left the Procuratie Nuove (mainly c17).
These were once homes of the Procuratori – important city officers.
Between them runs the Ala Napoleonica – a monument of the French
occupation. Among the statues on the façade are a number of Roman
emperors; the gap in the middle is supposed to have been intended for
Napoleon himself. The French continued the looting tradition (as did the

---

*The illustration (top) is of the Procuratie Nuove from the 'Gran Teatro di
Venezia'. It was begun by Scamozzi in 1586 as an echo of Sansovino's
Library and completed (gracefully altered) when Longhena refined the work
in 1640.*

*An engraving by Antonio Vissentini (1688–1782) of the Piazza from
Canaletto's drawing of 1754 shows the church of San Geminiano in the centre
background. This building was pulled down by the French to complete the
arcade, and to create in Napoleon's words 'the best drawing-room in Europe'.*

Germans in this century) even taking the bronze horses away to Paris. But they were first greeted as liberators from a useless and effete aristocracy. There is a song still popular in Venice – *La biondina in gondoleta*. (Bands in cafés will play it if asked.) Its heroine is the Countess Querini-Benzoni, a friend of Byron's. When Napoleon was approaching the city, she could be seen (it is said) dancing around a Tree of Liberty in front of the Basilica, dressed only in an Athenian tunic.

If you look back to the Porta della Carta (above the four porphyry Emperors) your will see a marble group representing the Doge Francesco Foscari kneeling before a Venetian lion reading a book. The original was destroyed in the rioting in 1797.

Eighteenth-century Venice was a paradigm of degradation. Her population had declined from 170,000 in her great days to 96,000 in 1797 (though the Venetian Association of Hairdressers still had 852 members). Her trade had vanished, her aristocracy was hopelessly effete, and she depended for her existence upon the tenuous good faith of her neighbours.

No wonder Napoleon swept her aside. The Venetians, temporising and vacillating offered him no real resistance, and he ended their Republic with a brusque gesture of dismissal: '*Io non voglio più Inquisitori, non voglio più Senato; sarò un Attila per lo stato Veneto*' – ' I want no more Inquisitors, no more Senate: I will be an Attila for the Venetian State.' The last of the Doges, limply abdicating, handed his ducal hat to his servant with the febrile comment: 'Take it away, we shan't be needing it again.' (The servant did what he was told, and kept it as a souvenir.) The golden horses of the Basilica, the lion from his pedestal in the Piazzetta, many of the treasures of St. Mark's, many of the pictures of the Doges' Palace, many precious books and documents – all were taken away to Paris, rather as so many of them had been stolen from Constantinople in the first place. Some diamonds from St. Mark's Treasury were set in Josephine's crown, and a large statue of Napoleon was erected on Sansovino's library building, opposite the Doge's Palace. The last ships of the Venetian Navy were seized to take part in an invasion of Ireland: but when this was cancelled they were sent instead to be sunk by Nelson at Aboukir.

The Great Council itself ended the aristocratic Government of Venice, by a vote of 512 yeas to 30 nays and 5 blanks, and for the words '*Pax Tibi Marce*', inscribed on the Venetian lion's open book, there was substituted the slogan 'Rights and Duties of Men and Citizens'. 'At last,' observed a gondolier in a phrase that has become proverbial – 'at last he's turned over a new leaf.'
MORRIS

The municipal band gives concerts in the Piazza in the evening.

I was often suddenly startled towards the end of my meal by the sound of my own overtures; then as I sat at the restaurant window giving myself up to impressions of the music, I did not know which dazzled me most, the incomparable Piazza magnificently illuminated and filled with countless numbers of moving people, or the music that seemed to be borne away in rustling glory to

Municipal band playing in the Piazza.

the winds. Only one thing was wanting that might certainly have been expected from an Italian audience: the people were gathered round the band in thousands listening most intently, but no two hands ever forgot themselves so far as to applaud, as the least sign of approbation of Austrian military music would have been looked upon as treason to the Italian Fatherland. All public life in Venice also suffered by this extraordinary rift between the general public and the authorities; this was peculiarly apparent in the relations of the population to the Austrian officers, who floated about publicly in Venice like oil on water. The populace, too, behaved with no less reserve, or one might even say hostility, to the clergy, who were for the most part of Italian origin. I saw a procession of clerics in the vestments passing along the Piazza San Marco accompanied by the people with unconcealed derision.

WAGNER

On the ground, immediately below, stands a stump of a porphyry column from a church in the Near East. It was one of two Proclamation Stones – from which the laws of the Republic were proclaimed to the people; the other is in the fruit market by the Rialto Bridge.

In the Piazza itself are, of course,

... the pigeons, most celebrated of the Venetian fauna. They are, by tradition, honoured and protected, and to have a roast pigeon lunch you must go down the road to Padua, or better still find yourself a musty trattoria among the Euganean Hills. Some say this is because Dandolo when he stormed Constantinople, sent back the news of the victory by carrier pigeon. Others believe that it arises from an old Palm Sunday custom, when a flock of pigeons was released in the Piazza, those that were caught by the populace being promptly eaten, those that escaped guaranteed permanent immunity – a ceremony that led in the long run, one pigeon looking very like another, to a safe conduct for them all. Whatever the truth, the pigeons have prospered. They survived some violent epidemics of pigeon-plague, picked up from carrion crows in the Levant, and nowadays never actually die, but merely go out into the lagoon and sink themselves. They are ... stuffed to excess by indulgent tourists ('those whose ambitions lean in that direction', as Baedeker loftily observes, 'may have themselves photographed covered with the birds').

MORRIS

But there is some evidence that the pigeon does not antedate the Austrian occupation: pictures of the Piazza during the time of the Republic show cats and dogs but not a single pigeon.

We now walk to the opposite end of the exterior gallery, past the horses. These are copies; the originals are kept inside.

For some decades they were kept at the Arsenal before being put in this place of honour where, about the middle of the XIV century, they were seen and

The north side of the Piazza showing much of the Procuratie Vecchie and, to the right, the Clock Tower where Walk 4 begins. The strolling players on their platform are dressed in the traditional Commedia del Arte costumes.

admired by Petrach, who was the first to write in praise of their beauty. They have undergone many restorations in succeeding periods and were traditionally considered to be Greek works of art of the IV–III century B.C. until recently they have been held by Eugenie Strong to be instead Roman works designed to decorate a triumphal arch. The four horses which came from the island of Chios, were sent to Constantinople where they were found by Doge Dandolo on the top of the high Tower of the Hippodrome.
LORENZETTI

[They] give an intensive animation to the sculptural decoration of St. Mark's. During the centuries when the art of creating equestrian statues was lost, these spirited horses must have been considered as miraculous works.
DECKER

Rising above the Procuratie Vecchie is the Clock Tower (Mauro Codussi, 1499). The clock, made by Paolo and his son Carlo Ranieri of Reggio, as the gilded inscription indicates, shows the time, date, phase of the moon and zodiac sign. The figures on top of the tower strike the hours; during

Ascension week other figures emerge from the doors on each side of the Madonna. On this side of the basilica is the Piazzetta dei Leoncini – the little lions are often ridden by children.

We now return to the interior of the church, at gallery level. The horses are to be seen in the Sala Cavalli Restaurati.

In San Marco we can see the mosaic developing from a Byzantine to a Western art. Byzantine buildings did not contain great areas of flat surface. 'Thus' says Demus,

> . . . what Greek decorators and their Western pupils had to learn in order to do justice to their tasks in Western buildings, was to marshal large programs and scenes on large surfaces, to work in widely differing scales, gigantic and almost miniature, and to instill a new rhythm into the rows of figures displayed on flat surfaces, in order to hold together the loosened, unframed compositions.

The mosaics are seen at their most brilliant on a bright day with sunlight entering through the west window. It is impossible to study them all: a representative selection may be made as follows:

Early c12: In the cupola nearest the w window – the cupola of the Pentecost – Byzantine in style, the Holy Ghost descends to the Apostles.

c12 to c13: Follow the gallery over the s side of the nave: stop at the point where it turns right into the right transept – in front of you (i.e. to the east), on the vault which crosses the transept, mosaics in Ravenna style. Bottom left: *Jesus enters Jerusalem.*

Early c13: From here you can see some of the figures of the central cupola (The Ascension dome): this is a Venetian version of Byzantine mannerist style remarkable, as Demus says, for its 'agitated movements, swirling draperies with plastic islands surrounded by flowing folds, distorted faces and dynamic compositions'.

> The arrival of this agitated style with its soft-flowing forms coincided with the activity of an artist of great stature, the master of the Ascension dome, a Byzantine-trained Venetian, as it seems, whose style quickly became the strongest and the most expansive element in the art of Venice. He not only dominated mosaic painting in San Marco itself and in Torcello, but his style of composition and modeling set the tune for fresco painting as well; some of the frescoes in the crypt of Aquileia cathedral are paraphrases of mosaics in San Marco. What is, however, more astonishing still, is that some of his figures, those of the Virtues in the Ascension dome,[1] which belong to the most spirited creations of late twelfth century mosaic painting, were translated more than a generation later into sculptural reliefs to decorate one of the arches of the main porch of the church[2]; even sculpture in the round was inspired by works of this style, for one of the angels placed (in the early thirteenth century) under the central dome of San Marco, to stress the Parousia or Judgment aspect of the

Ascension,[3] is a translation into three-dimensional sculpture of one of the tuba-sounding mosaic angels on the west wall of Torcello cathedral.
DEMUS

On your way to this spot you passed the *Prayer in the Garden* on your right. It is the lower scene on the wall of the s aisle. Here the Byzantine background has begun to make way for landscape.

Late c13: Turn now into the s transept. On the w wall the lower scene tells the legend of the *Finding of the Body of St Mark*.

In this is represented with ingenious art, the interior of the Basilica, where the episodes here described took place. The tradition relates how in 1063, when the building of the new temple was begun, the body of the Evangelist was, during the building, jealously hidden; afterwards the traces were lost and every search having proved fruitless, special fasts and services were held. In the scene at the left: (a) *The Doge, the Signoria, the Clergy and the People take part in the services celebrated in St. Mark's for help to find the body of the Evangelist.* After this, by a wonderful miracle, St. Mark revealed the place where his body had been deposited and from the pilaster beside the present Altar of the Sacrament an arm appeared destroying part of the marble facing which hid it. Indeed in the mosaic to the right, (b) *The Bishop, the Doge, the Procuratori and the People* are present in surprise at the miracle. This happened, according to the pious tradition, on the 25th June 1094.
LORENZETTI

Go to the end of the walkway; if you turn round and look over the balustrading down into the church you will be facing the Altar of the Sacrament. On the pier to the left of this altar is the pillar in question: a panel and a lamp mark the spot.

One other area (mid c13) merits special mention: it is the arch immediately to the east of the Pentecost cupola. *Jesus descending into Limbo* – the upper scene – can be seen from this side: it is worth going round to the other side to view the *Crucifixion*. The great period of mosaic appears to have ended with the c13 (but see the c14 mosaics in the chapel of St Isidore, mentioned on p.40).

The walkways we have used are what remain of the galleries, designed according to the Eastern custom, to accommodate the women during the ceremonies. The galleries on either side of the nave have parapets made up of carved and pierced panels c6–c11. The endless variety of columns and capitals can also be seen from here.

---

[1] on the eastern side of the dome.
[2] Compare the mosaic 'Fortitudo' with the bottom relief on the arch, and the mosaic 'Eperatia' with the figure on the arch fourth from the bottom – MG.   [3] above and to the right of the choir screen.

Take the stairs down to the ground floor and return to the Piazza. The base of the central standard is a convenient resting place. On it is a small profile of a c16 Doge, in the shape of a medallion. The central arch of the basilica displays a miniature history of the development of Gothic sculpture: the inmost arch is early c13, the middle later and the outer arch early c14.

Now the first broad characteristic of the building, and the root of nearly every other important peculiarity in it, is its confessed *incrustation*. It is the purest example in Italy of the great school of architecture in which the ruling principle is the incrustation of brick with more precious materials, and it is necessary, before we proceed to criticise any one of its arrangements, that the reader should carefully consider the principles which are likely to have influenced, or might legitimately influence, the architects of such a school, as distinguished from those whose designs are to be executed in massive materials. This incrusted school appears insincere at first to a Northern builder, because, accustomed to build with solid blocks of freestone, he is in the habit of supposing the external superficies of a piece of masonry to be some criterion of its thickness. But, as soon as he gets acquainted with the incrusted style, he will find that the Southern builders had no intention to deceive him. He will see that every slab of facial marble is fastened to the next by a confessed *rivet*, and that the joints of the armour are so visibly and openly accommodated to the contours of the substance within that he has no more right to complain of treachery than a savage would have, who, for the first time in his life seeing a man in armour, had supposed him to be made of solid steel. Acquaint him with the customs of chivalry, and with the uses of the coat of mail, and he ceases to accuse of dishonesty either the panoply or the knight.
RUSKIN

Venice took her role as heir to a part of the Roman Empire very seriously. And this accounts for the method of decorating the exterior of San Marco – and much else besides – in Veneto-Byzantine architecture. Many of the elements in the decorative scheme are Byzantine – notably the use of sculpture as surface ornament and not, as was normal elsewhere in Europe, to express the structure. But no parallel to the abundance of columns and marble cladding is to be found on any other Byzantine building of this period. Archaeologists have discovered behind these decorations the mid-twelfth-century brick façade which, somewhat surprisingly, was decorated not with round headed but with pointed arches and arcading. Thus, when the rest of Europe was developing the Gothic style, Venice was turning back to the ancient world for inspiration. Apparently this lavish use of marble was a conscious attempt to revive the splendours of ancient Rome – though the architect looked back no further than to the Early Christian period. It was, however, by such a return to a form of classicism – also reflected in domestic architecture where the two-story portico became popular – that Venice triumphantly proclaimed her succession to the Roman Empire, if no more than a 'quarter and half a quarter' of it.
    On the main façade the carvings are arranged in a clear iconographic programme to stress the church's function as a national shrine. The basic construction is that of a vast triumphal arch with five openings. In the spandrels

between the arches there are six relief carvings. That on the far left represents
Hercules carrying the Erymanthean boar, a Roman work of the third century,
that on the far right is a Venetian imitation of it carved one thousand years later.
Hercules was supposed to have been the original tribal hero of the Veneti from
whom the Venetians claimed descent, he had an allegorical role as the Saviour
conquering evil, he was also recognised as the type of hero protector. The next
two reliefs, reading inwards – Venetian carvings after Byzantine prototypes –
represent the Virgin and the Archangel of the Annunciation both of whom were
regarded as protectors of the ruler of the state. The two central reliefs represent
Saints who were warriors and thus the protectors of warriors, St. Demetrius and
St. George – the first a late twelfth-century Byzantine carving and the second a
Venetian imitation of it . . .
HONOUR

It is worth looking closely at the arch at the extreme left of the façade
(the Porta di San Alipio). The concave mosaic, c13, shows the church as it
was then, and the body of St Mark being carried into it. Needing a relic
and a patron saint of more consequence than the Greek San Todero, the
Venetians stole the body from Alexandria in 829. The other mosaics were
later replaced, but most of them can be seen in Bellini's *Procession* in the
Accademia (p.87). Below are five pierced screens of Byzantine window
form. The lintel appears to be c5 or c6 Syrian work.

> . . . the reliefs of the lintel . . . consist of eleven pieces which were arranged
> differently at different periods, so that it is impossible in their present location to
> determine the order in which they were set in the thirteenth century. They were
> certainly in their present place at the end of the fifteenth century since they
> figure in Gentile Bellini's rendering of the façade . . . The end-piece on the left
> appears to be in its original place, since the irregularly inclined pillar that frames
> it on the left-hand side fits exactly the slant of the adjoining architrave . . . .
> This piece with the standing figure of a priest carrying a *turibulum* (censer)
> differs in no way from the end-piece on the right-hand side, and the heads of the
> two figures – to say nothing of the framing pillars – match the bearded heads of
> other figures of the lintel so closely that it is difficult to imagine that the various
> pieces belong to different hands or periods.
>
> Nevertheless . . . the cycle does not make sense iconographically. The true
> difficulty begins . . . with the Gospel scenes. Their sequence (Annunciation to the
> Shepherds, Adoration of the Magi, and Miracle of Cana) can by no means be
> regarded as a self-contained cycle. They can only be fragments or remnants of a
> large ensemble, or, at best, the beginning of a cycle. Moreover, one of the three
> scenes, the Annunciation to the Shepherds, requires a continuation on its left.
> This scene cannot be complete, since it includes the Child in the manger,
> flanked by the ox and the ass, but neither the Virgin nor St. Joseph; these latter
> must have been represented in the adjoining compartment.
>
> It is furthermore possible to state that some of these reliefs were originally
> attached to a curved surface, since the larger scenic reliefs are unmistakably
> convex.

... we see in the lintel the remnants of an Early Christian work, restored, reworked, and completed in the thirteenth century. It is the extensive reworking which makes it well-nigh impossible to establish the real date of each single piece.

DEMUS

We can enter by the centre portal. Some sculptural detail has been lost to pollution, notably the tradesmen's tools, inside the outer arch. Within the atrium, on the floor, marble mosaics c11–c12 and a red lozenge of stone, traditionally the spot where Barbarossa submitted to Pope Alexander III in 1177. On the ceiling, fine c13 mosaics: the last cupola on the right is the earliest and best preserved. The series begins there, with a mosaic which depicts *Creation of the World*. The story of Noah is told in the mosaics of the arch to the north of the *Creation* cupola. The close connexion between mosaic and sculpture in this epoch can be seen comparing the depiction of the sawing of boards in the outer arch of the central portal with the mosaic showing the building of Noah's Ark.

It has been known since the eighties of the last century, when J. J. Tikkanen published his discovery, that the Old Testament mosaics of the Narthex or Atrium of San Marco in Venice are, at least in their greater part, more or less faithful copies of an illuminated manuscript of the type of the Cotton Genesis in the British Museum. It would, of course, be wrong to expect from the Venetian mosaicists of the thirteenth century slavish reproductions of their more than 700 year old models; Tikkanen has shown that they retained a certain independence in the selection of the scenes to be included in their programme and that they altered the prototypes as regards position and spacing of figures, coloring, and movement, even going so far as to break up some of the old compositions and making up new ones from their component parts. Forlati's soundings make it likely that the preparatory brush drawings (sinopie) were closer to the model than the finished mosaics. But even so, the mosaics are close enough to dispel any doubt that the Venetian mosaicists of the thirteenth century had both the intention and the ability to bring about in their work a close approximation to early sixth century iconography and style.

All this goes to show that there was a strong archaizing current in Venetian art, manifesting itself in the collecting and exhibiting of early spoils, in the copying and imitating of early Christian works of painting and sculpture; a current that must have been strong enough to result in the unparalleled ability of Venetian masters to speak fluently, as it were, a foreign language of style and meaning. Now, what can have been the driving forces behind this movement which goes far beyond the usual trends of archaism in medieval art? The answer lies in the very special situation of Venice, both geographically and historically. Venice had, to begin with, no hinterland, at least in the earlier stages of its civic development. No deeply ingrained tendencies were present which might have prevented the Venetian artists from giving themselves over to the imitation of foreign and antiquated forms. But Venice lacked more than a hinterland: it lacked a past. It had appeared comparatively late in the history of the Mediterranean world. Being without a past was, however, in the Middle Ages very much like being a man without his shadow – like Chamisso's Peter Schlemihl. To cure this defect, the statesmen of the Middle Ages developed a remedy – the same that is being used even today by states and individuals: if one had no past, one could always fake one. In a way, this was easier than it is now. The forgers of the Middle Ages were not hampered as we are by existing records, proofs, and counterproofs. They could fake freely and to measure.

This is what the Venetians did, at least from the eleventh century onwards, when the need arose to bolster up their slowly developed independence, especially in ecclesiastic matters. An intricate web of forgeries was fabricated (and borrowed) by which Grado, the Metropolitan See of the National Church of Venice, was made to appear as the legitimate successor of Aquileia which, in its turn, traced its origin, by forged documents and legends, back to St. Hermagoras and through him, to the Holy Mark himself. The church of the Evangelist, the very center of Venetian political and religious life, could not be antedated: the date of the transfer of the Patron Saint's relics from Alexandria to Venice in 828–829 and of the subsequent erection of his first church in Rialto was too well established; but the church could be given an aura of venerability by making it a 'simile' of the old and venerable Church of the Holy Apostles in Constantinople where, as in San Marco itself, the 'pignora imperii' were kept. Venice resurrected with this also a time-hallowed Italian tradition that can be followed back to St. Ambrose's foundation of Apostles' churches from Milan to Rouen, Aquileia, and Fondi.

The building of the first San Marco, from 830 onwards, after the pattern of the Holy Apostles was, as far as we know, the earliest instance of conscious archaism in Venice. The second building, at the end of the eleventh century, improved on its predecessor which had, in all probability, wooden cupolas. Now, from 1063 onwards, the church was vaulted and built in brick as one of the most successful imitations of a famous model that the history of architecture knows. But, even so, it was not perfect: it lacked a decoration to vie with the mosaics of the Constantinople church. The early thirteenth century remedied this.
DEMUS

Right at the opposite end of the atrium (past the postcard stall and round the corner to the right) is the Moses cupola. The ten scenes depict incidents from the life of Moses in a manner quite remote from the pseudo-archaic Genesis cupola.

The main door into the church has two niches on either side. Demus takes the mosaics in these niches as examples of the 'ascetic' style, in which the influence of Byzantium was first transmitted to Venice in the second half of the c11.

Straight lines, seeking the vertical, articulate the austere draperies of these figures; the only features to enliven this pattern are folded seams zigzagging obliquely across the legs, one of which is usually accentuated, by framing contours and a triangular shadow under the knee.

The style appears in Venice in several of its varieties, one of which can be seen in the apostles of the main apse of Torcello cathedral, also of the second half of c11, a rather rich, overcharged version, which recalls the heavy, provincial idiom of the Kiev mosaics. The second phase, at the turn of c11, is represented by the four monumental figures in the main apse[1].
DEMUS

Let us enter the church. It is lost in still deeper twilight, to which the eye must be accustomed for some moments before the form of the building can be traced; and then there opens before us a vast cave, hewn out into the form of a Cross, and divided into shadowy aisles by many pillars. Round the domes of its roof the light enters only through narrow apertures like large stars; and here and there a ray or two from some far-away casement wanders into the darkness, and casts a narrow phosphoric stream upon the waves of marble that heave and fall in a thousand colours along the floor. What else there is of light is from torches, or silver lamps, burning ceaselessly in the recesses of the chapels; the roof sheeted with gold, and the polished walls covered with alabaster, give back at every curve and angle some feeble gleaming to the flames; and the glories round the heads of the sculptured saints flash out upon us as we pass them and sink again into the gloom. Under foot and over head, a continual succession of crowded imagery, one picture passing into another, as in a dream; forms beautiful and terrible mixed together – dragons and serpents, and ravening beasts of prey, and graceful birds that in the midst of them drink from running fountains and feed from bases of crystal; the passions and the pleasures of human life symbolised together, and the mystery of its redemption; for the mazes of interwoven lines and changeful pictures lead always at last to the Cross, lifted and carved in every place and upon every stone; sometimes with the serpent of eternity wrapt round it, sometimes with doves beneath its arms, and sweet herbage growing forth from its feet; but conspicuous most of all on the great rood that crosses the church before the altar, raised in bright blazonry against the shadow of the apse.
RUSKIN

In the use of significant geometrical figures – the square, the circle and the cross – and the mystic relationship between the proportions, it answers the Byzantine passion for symbolism and the Byzantine belief in the laws of harmony and sanctity of mathematics, 'the highest of the sciences'. Nevertheless, it is essentially a Byzantine church with Italian decorations and nothing like it was ever built in the eastern Empire. The original effect was quite different and much more outspokenly Byzantine. There were many more windows and there were galleries above the aisles so that light flooded into the whole central area making a much stronger contrast with the surrounding shade. With their passion for surface decoration, the Venetians walled up many windows to make room for additional mosaics. This made the area under the galleries so dangerously dark that their floors had to be removed, leaving only the strange cat-walks you see today.
HONOUR

---

[1]See p.40.

It is all so quiet and sad and faded and yet all so brilliant and living. The strange
figures in the mosaic pictures, bending with the curve of niche and vault, stare
down through the glowing dimness; the burnished gold that stands behind them
catches the light on its little uneven cubes. St. Mark's owes nothing of its
character to the beauty of proportion or perspective; there is nothing grandly
balanced or far-arching; there are no long lines nor triumphs of the perpendicular.
The church arches indeed, but arches like a dusky cavern. Beauty of surface, of
tone, of detail, of things near enough to touch and kneel upon and lean against –
it is from this the effect proceeds. In this sort of beauty the place is incredibly
rich, and you may go there every day and find afresh some lurking pictorial
nook. You grow fond even of the old benches of red marble, partly worn away
by the breeches of many generations and attached to the base of those wide
pilasters of which the precious plating, delightful in its faded brownness, with a
faint grey bloom upon it, bulges and yawns a little with honourable age.
HENRY JAMES

Beside the first column on the right there is a porphyry stoup supported
on a Roman fragment c2. Through the door behind is the Baptistry, and
opposite the entrance the funeral monument of Doge Andrea Dandolo
mid c14 – see the reliefs on the front of the sarcophagi (the dove
especially). Turning right we reach the Capella Zen, remodelled c16
(restored, Save Venice Inc). On each side of the altar is a c13 lion in red
marble. On the wall to the right of the altar is an early Christian carving
of the c4. The mosaics here and in the Baptistry are c14; the figures
continue to be garbed in the traditional Byzantine manner. The figure of
Salome by contrast (on the left of the lunette over the entrance door)
owes more to the Gothic; she is pictured as a fashionably dressed woman
of the mid c14.

In the s transept is the entrance to the Treasury (*Tesoro*). It contains a
number of objects, mainly of Byzantine origin.

. . . it is important to remember that in Byzantium, as in China, there was no
dividing line between the major and minor arts. It would not be going too far to
say that all Byzantine arts, including architecture, aspired to the jewel-like
delicacy and richness of an enamelled reliquary. In the Treasury there is a
twelfth-century reliquary of gold and silver in the form of a church[1] – it should
be regarded as an ideal of what a church should look like rather than the model
of a building. Had Byzantine architects been able to build with gold and silver
and precious stones they would undoubtedly have done so.
HONOUR

A combined ticket gives admission to the Pala d'Oro also. This is reached
via the ticket desk to the right of the high altar. On the way, pause in

front of the rood screen to look at the little arches and pilasters (c11) which decorate the base of the chancel.

The c10–c12 enamels of the Pala d'Oro are mostly Byzantine; many were looted from Constantinople in 1204, at the time of the Fourth Crusade. They are set in a screen which reached its present form in c14 (restored mid c19, and recently by the Association France-Italie). They repay detailed examination. Demus remarks on the spiral whirls on the knees of the standing and seated figures. These recur in Romanesque stone carving, but seem, he says, so much more 'natural' in cloisonné enamel. Demus also comments on the four monumental mosaic figures in the main apse with the 'ascetic'-style figures we saw in the niches beside the main door. The apse figures, dating from the turn of c11,

> . . . are livelier, more personal as it were, and freer in attitude, gesture and
> expression. Contours, seams and folds are somewhat curvilinear and the
> modelling is more comprehensive, giving body and weight to the figure as a
> whole.
> DEMUS

If you stand in front of the high altar you will see on the vault over the gallery a series of mosaics illustrating episodes from the life of St Mark. Demus takes the last – the body of the saint welcomed by the Doge, clergy and people – as an example of the archaising trends and tendencies of the mid c13 in Venice: it is an adapted copy of a c6 mosaic, the dedicatory panel of Justinian, in San Vitale, Ravenna. On either side of the chancel (behind you at this point) are two little galleries – *cantorie* – decorated with c16 High Renaissance reliefs by Sansovino – only really visible if the day is bright.

Over the high altar is the richly decorated ciborium supported on four columns. These are examples of the same archaising tendency: they appear to be works of early Christian character both as regards style and iconography, but certainly the front pair and probably also the back pair are now believed to be works of the c13. To the left of the high altar, a fine curved bronze door by Sansovino.

We emerge into the N transept; on the E side, the altar of the Virgin (c17) contains an image of the Virgin called *La Nicopeia* also taken by the Venetians from Byzantium at the time of the Fourth Crusade. Beyond, at the end of the N transept, bronze c14 gates lead to the Chapel of St Isidore. This chapel has a very fine cycle of c14 mosaics, hardly touched by restoration, depicting events in the life of the Saint.

Beside the chapel of St Isidore is the chapel of the Madonna of the Males (Mascoli). The relief on the altar front – two angels bearing censers

– shows Tuscan influence. The mosaics (c15) are late but elegant.

We return to the transept. Beside the rood screen is a late c13 pulpit on which is superimposed a pulpit of later date owing much to the South Italian and Islamic styles. The mosaics of the easternmost dome show a multiplicity of styles and are plainly the work of more than one artist.

> One of the artists copied the much older figures of the apse, another developed a highly mannered, jagged style, and a third (and probably a fourth) produced a somewhat provincial version of the current mannerism of the second half of the twelfth century with its overemphasis on plastic differentiation.
> DEMUS

> There was so little unity of planning that the two transept domes were filled with what appear as leftovers from the overall decorative scheme, miniature-like scenes of the legend of St. John the Evangelist in the north dome and four lonely figures of saints in the south dome.
> DEMUS

We leave by the N aisle. On the way out we walk over some fine mosaics of birds.

We now come back into the Piazza. This is a good moment for a rest – perhaps some coffee – and some more general observations.

> The palaces of Venice, when they need support, are strengthened by the injection of concrete into their foundations, as a dentist squeezes a filling into a rotting but still useful tooth: this entails the building of a water-tight caisson around the house, and the Municipality contributes half the cost. About thirty of the Grand Canal palaces have been treated. The Basilica is constantly attended by its own private consultant, the resident engineer, successor to a long line of Architects to St. Mark's. This learned and devoted man knows every inch of his church, and spends his life devising ways of strengthening it without spoiling its antique irregularities. He has a staff of nearly forty men working all the year round, and a mosaic workshop manned by twelve skilled craftsmen. He is always experimenting and has in particular perfected a means of replacing broken chips of mosaic in the ceiling by cutting through the masonry above and inserting the precious fragments from behind.
> MORRIS

> Venice rose and lives on the water: for this reason its water-ways are as important in its life as the network of its streets. The internal Rii (canals), filled with shallow water about two metres deep and not very wide (from 4 to 5 metres), used by gondolas, launches, and shallow draft boats, are spanned by *Bridges* that connect both banks, often flanked by long narrow streets – the fondamenta that run close to the foundations of the houses. The bridges,

originally flat with planks, suitable for horse traffic, a means of transport still used by Venetians up to the fifteenth century, then later built of stone and brick, arched and with balustrades. The two largest tracts of water are, however, called Canals: the *Giudecca Canal* which is very large and the *Grand Canal* which, with a double curve divides the city into two parts anciently called: *de citra e de ultra*, that is on this and that side of the Canal in respect to the Piazza San Marco; besides being used by craft of every kind and shape, it is spanned by three large bridges: the *Rialto Bridge*, the oldest (XVI cent.) almost half-way down it, made of stone, the Academy Bridge in wood, and the Railway Bridge in stone (Eugenio Miozzi 1932). The two shores are, besides, connected by numerous ferries, mooring places for gondolas and for the carrying of people from one side of the canal to the other.

Although the water-ways have, of necessity, been developed, it must not be thought, as is erroneously done by non-Venetians, that to go round Venice one has absolutely to use boats. On the contrary many picturesque and characteristic corners hidden in the interior of the city can only be reached by penetrating the intricate maze of its alleyways: those are the *calli*, some of which are so narrow as to allow one person to pass with difficulty, and made still more dark by buildings jutting out (to gain space), sustained by wooden joists, the *barbacani*, which almost form a covering to them. Quite often, however, the maze of alleys is interrupted by spacious areas of open ground, the *campi*, so called because they were once grassy; these generally stretch out before a church and one or more *vere da pozzo* (well-heads) are almost never lacking. The one of San Marco was called a *piazza* because it is more beautiful and spacious, and the two smaller ones adjoining it *piazzette*, just as only the embankment that runs along beside the Pool of San Marco was given the name *Riva degli Schiavoni*. *Corti* and *campielli* are smaller open spaces, less than the *campi*. The medium width streets, flanked with houses and shops are called *ruga* or *rughetta*. A *rio terrà* is, instead, a *rio interrato* (filled-in canal) and turned into a street. The first streets to be paved are called *salizzade*. *Ramo* is a small trace of a street connecting two bigger streets. Little sorts of ponds where the rain-water stagnated, later filled in, were called by the very old name of *piscine*. Last of all the *sottoportici* are the covered passageways or more or less narrow passages, opened for the convenience of the public, beneath private homes.

Apart from a few exceptions the old nomenclature of the streets has been maintained more or less unaltered. The characteristic denominations in Venetian dialect have been preserved, written in big black letters on a plaster background. They are names derived from the neighbourhoods, very often of the Patron Saint of the parish, so that we might say that by wandering round Venice we can learn and repeat most of the religious calendar. Sometimes these names recall the aristocratic family that lived nearby or some characteristic oddity of the spot. At times, however, the names have suffered strange incomprehensible transformations such as: *San Trovaso*, a combination of two names of Gervasio and Protasio; *San Stae*, a transformation of Sant' Eustachio; *San Marcuola*, the fusion of the two names Sant Ermagora and Fortunato; *San Lio*, an abbreviation of San Leone; *Sant' Aponal*, from Sant' Apollinare etc.

LORENZETTI

We now walk towards the Lagoon, into the Piazzetta. The third of the Piazzetta next to the Ducal Palace was called the Broglio: in republican times, patricians walked here, and persons seeking favours would kiss their sleeves. Our word *imbroglio* comes from the intrigues which began in that way. The c16 building on the right is Sansovino's Library. It reminds us that the Venetians were not intellectuals: Venice was famous for its printers, not writers. The last thing suggested by this splendid and showy civic monument is anything which could be described as 'bookish'.

Sansovino had completely adapted his style and manner to the genius of the place, the brilliant light of Venice, which is reflected by the lagoons, and dazzles the eyes by its splendour. It may seem a little pedantic to anatomize such a festive and simple building, but to look at it carefully may help us to see how skilled these masters were in weaving a few simple elements into ever-new patterns. The lower storey, then, with its vigorous Doric order of columns, is in the most orthodox classical manner. Sansovino had closely followed the rules of building which the Colosseum exemplified. He adhered to the same tradition when he arranged the upper storey in the Ionic order, carrying a so-called 'attic' crowned with a balustrade and topped by a row of statues. But instead of letting the arched openings between the orders rest on pillars, as had been the case on the Colosseum, Sansovino supported them by another set of small Ionic columns, and thus achieved a rich effect of interlocked orders. With his balustrade, garlands and sculptures he gave the building something of the appearance of tracery such as had been used on the Gothic façades of Venice.
GOMBRICH

The library contains book bindings, illuminated codexes, and early printed books. In the vestibule, Titian's *Wisdom*.

In painting . . . a greater effect of reality is chiefly a matter of light and shadow, to be obtained only by considering the canvas as an enclosed space, filled with light and air, through which the objects are seen. There is more than one way of getting this effect, but Titian attains it by the almost total suppression of outlines, by the harmonizing of his colours, and by the largeness and vigour of his brushwork. In fact, the old Titian was, in his way of painting, remarkably like the best French masters at the end of the nineteenth century. This makes him only the more attractive, particularly when with handling of this kind he combined the power of creating forms of beauty such as he has given us in 'Wisdom'.
BERENSON

The hall is remarkable for its ceiling of real gold. Pictures on each side of the door: Veronese, *Two Philosophers*.

If you look at the Library from the waterfront you will see to the left of it the façade of the former Mint (Zecca). It was designed by Sansovino as a two-storey building. The third, added over a decade later, is weaker, and fits awkwardly with the end façade of the Library. The ground floor incorporated – behind the rusticated arches – cheese and salami shops which existed on the site. The gold was minted on the floor above. The word 'sequin' appears to be derived from the *Zecchini* – gold ducats – minted in Venice. A collection of Venetian coins is housed in the Correr Museum. The Zecca contains ancient books and manuscripts.

We now turn to the façade of the Ducal Palace. Atmospheric pollution and pigeon droppings have casued a good deal of decay to the surface of the stone.

> The outer walls rest upon the sturdy pillars of open colonnades, which have a more stumpy appearance than was intended, owing to the raising of the pavement in the piazza.
> HARE

On the corner – *Adam and Eve* in high relief. Ruskin takes the head of Adam as an example of sculpture intended to be seen from a distance.

> It is only at the height of 17 or 18 feet above the eye; nevertheless, the sculptor felt it was no use to trouble himself about drawing the corners of the mouth, or the lines of the lips, delicately, at that distance; his object has been to mark them clearly, and to prevent accidental shadows from concealing them, or altering their expression. The lips are cut thin and sharp, so that their line cannot be mistaken, and a good deep drill-hole struck into the angle of the mouth; the eye is anxious and questioning, and one is surprised, from below, to perceive a kind of darkness in the iris of it, neither like colour, nor like a circular furrow. The expedient can only be discovered by ascending to the level of the head; it is one which would have been quite inadmissible except in distant work, six drill-holes cut into the iris, round a central one for the pupil.
> RUSKIN

Pass in front of the Ducal Palace: over the column to the left of the central door, a round spandril decoration of fine geometric design. There is another over the column third from the right. Similar marble decorations appear to have been envisaged over the other columns (noticeably on the Piazzetta façade). Continuing in front of the palace, we come to the bridge. Byron's line beginning the fourth canto of *Childe Harold, 'I stood in Venice, on the Bridge of Sighs'* presumably means that

The crenellated buildings which housed both the department of health and the public granary, in this plate from the 'Gran Teatro di Venezia', were pulled down during the Napoleonic occupation. The site (now a public garden) can be seen in the background of the 1843 lithograph below.

he stood in Venice on this bridge – the Bridge of Straw (Ponte della
Paglia) – and contemplated the Bridge of Sighs. The view is deservedly
famous. The bridge is grimly elegant: it contains dark passages, lit by
gratings, connecting the palace with the prison. It is worth going over the
Straw Bridge, turning immediately left and looking across the water.

> . . . the best bit of Renaissance design in Venice, the side of the Ducal Palace
> next the Bridge of Sighs, owes great part of its splendour to its foundation, faced
> with large flat dogteeth, each about a foot wide in the base, with their points
> truncated, and alternating with cavities, which are their own negatives or casts.
> RUSKIN

From here you can also see the relief of the *Drunkenness of Noah* on the
corner of the Palazzo; two sons cover his nakedness, the other son is
represented on the other side of the arch.

This and the *Adam and Eve* are credited to Raverti, the architect of
Milan cathedral (as are the more realistic of the carvings on the capitals).
Both these reliefs, Lauritzen says, had an allegorical function: they
represented two aspects of good government – its severity being
represented by the punishment of Adam and Eve, and its mercy by the
compassion of Shem and Japheth.

Now come back in front of the Palazzo and return to the Piazzetta: the
Gothic reliefs on the capitals merit, as Ruskin advised, careful examin-
ation (though a number of them have been replaced by late c19
facsimiles). Ruskin takes the fourth capital from the *Drunkenness of
Noah* corner as illustrative of his general view of the nobility of High
Gothic Venice and the degeneracy of everything that came with the
Renaissance. He is stimulating, even if not convincing. The fourth
capital

> . . . has three children. The eastern one is defaced: the one in front holds a small
> bird, whose plumage is beautifully indicated, in its right hand; and with its left
> holds up half a walnut, showing the nut inside: the third holds a fresh fig, cut
> through, showing the seeds[1].
>   The hair of all the three children is differently worked; the first has
> luxuriant flowing hair, and a double chin; the second, light flowing hair falling
> in pointed locks on the forehead; the third crisp curling hair, deep cut with drill
> holes.

---

[1] Ruskin mentions the repairs which the palace was undergoing when he spent the
winter in Venice and the scaffolding which had been erected for that purpose. He
must have seen these seeds by climbing the scaffolding.

Drunkenness of Noah.

This capital has been copied on the Renaissance side of the palace[1] only with such changes in the ideal of the children as the workmen thought expedient and natural. It is highly interesting to compare the child of the fourteenth with the child of the fifteenth century. The early heads are full of youthful life, playful, humane, affectionate, beaming with sensation and vivacity, but with much manliness and firmness also, not a little cunning, and some cruelty perhaps, beneath all; the features small and hard, and the eyes keen. There is the making of rough and great men in them. But the children of the fifteenth century are dull smooth-faced dunces, without a single meaning line in the fatness of their stolid cheeks; and, although, in the vulgar sense, as handsome as the other children are ugly, capable of becoming nothing but perfumed coxcombs.
RUSKIN

Under the arcading on the Piazzetta side is an illuminating tablet[2]. The first duty of the Venetian nobleman was to the State: if he failed in his duty he was punished. In no other country in the world, as Hare remarks, does one see tablets set up in the walls of public edifices, with inscriptions which do not praise but condemn. Here we read that Girolamo Loredan and Giovanni Contarini were banished for having ceded the fortress of Tenedo to the Turks, with its arms and munitions, causing grave injury to Christianity, and to their country.

At the end of the arcade we come once again to the Porta della Carta: on the right, the *Judgment of Solomon* on the pillar and the *Law-givers* on the capital below; beyond, the c15 Giants' Stairs – a magnificent gesture in incrusted marble, now topped by Sansovino's guardian figures of the 'giants' Mars and Neptune, monumental in size, but in relaxed mannerist attitudes. We enter the courtyard through the Foscari Porch (Arco Foscari): the charming Adam and Eve figures are bronze copies of statues by Antonio Rizzo, the architect of the Giants' Stairs. It is only fair to say at this stage that the inside of the Palazzo (open **8.30–18.00**) is a bit of an ordeal; there are however some fine things, and by being extremely selective, I think it is possible to enjoy them.

Ducal Palace

The route through the palace begins with the Golden Staircase and leads through the Doge's Apartments – on right at first landing (if closed, continue to second landing and Square Hall, below). In the Hall of the Philosophers, on the staircase (through little door on right) Titian: frescoe, *Saint Christopher*

---

[1] The side facing the Piazzetta. The capital is next to the last on the extreme left.
[2] At the time of writing it has been removed for restoration.

The interior court of the Ducal Palace in 1741 by Michele Marieschi (1710–43).

The next three rooms of the Doge's Apartments comprise the picture gallery, and contain
Giovanni Bellini: *Jesus supported by Virgin and Saints* (now attributed mainly to Gentile Bellini)

The Church from the first took account of the influence of colour as well as of music upon the emotions. From the earliest times it employed mosaic and painting to enforce its dogmas and relate its legends, not merely because this was the only means of reaching people who could neither read nor write but also because it instructed them in a way which, far from leading to critical enquiry, was peculiarly capable of being used as an indirect stimulus to moods of devotion and contrition. Next to the finest mosaics of the first centuries, the early works of Giovanni Bellini, the greatest Venetian master of the 15th century, best fulfil this religious intention. Painting has in his life-time reached a point where the difficulties of technique no longer stood in the way of the expression of profound emotion. No one can look at Bellini's pictures of the Dead Christ upheld by the Virgin or angels without being put into a mood of deep contrition, nor at his earlier Madonnas without a thrill of awe and reverence. And Giovanni Bellini

does not stand alone. His contemporaries Gentile Bellini and Vivarini, Crivalli
and Cima da Conegliano all began by painting in the same spirit, and produced
almost the same effect.
BERENSON

Carpaccio: *Winged Lion Passant*
On the right of the Carpaccio, c15 bust of Doge Francesco Foscari,
remnant of the group over the Porta della Carta.
The route returns to the Golden Staircase. Go up the stairs (restored,
I F M) to the Square Hall and continue to the Hall of the Four Doors, in
which the centre picture on the entrance wall is
Titian: *Doge Grimani Kneeling before Faith*

Over the window on the canal
G. B. Tiepolo: *Neptune bearing Treasures to Venice*
The original is now displayed on a stand, its place over the window being
taken by a copy.

The next room is the hall of the Ante-College, in which, on wall facing
windows,
Veronese: *Rape of Europa*
and on wall beside window
Tintoretto: *Bacchus and Ariadne*

The College Hall, next, has a spectacular ceiling.

> The roof is entirely by Paul Veronese, and the traveller who really loves
> painting ought to get leave to come to this room whenever he chooses, and
> should pass the sunny summer mornings there again and again . . . He will not
> otherwise enter so deeply into the heart of Venice.
> RUSKIN

Over the door by which we leave,
Tintoretto: *Marriage of Saint Catherine.*

It is some way to the Great Council Hall. On the wall over the rostrum
Tintoretto: *Paradiso* (restored, Save Venice Inc).

> I believe this is, on the whole, Tintoret's 'chef-d'œuvre'; though it is so vast that
> no one takes the trouble to read it, and therefore less wonderful pictures are
> preferred to it . . . . In the Paradise of Tintoret, the angel is seen in the distance
> driving Adam and Eve out of the garden. Not, for Tintoret, the leading to the

The Doge Alvise Mocenigo IV receiving the foreign ambassadors in the Sala Collegio, 1763. An engraving by Giovanni Battista Brustolon from a drawing by Canaletto.

gate with consolation and counsel. His strange ardour of conception is seen here as everywhere. Full speed they fly, the angel and the human creatures; the angel, wrapt in an orb of light, floats on, stooped forward in his fierce flight, and does not touch the ground; the chastised creatures rush before him in abandoned terror. All this might have been invented by another, though in other hands it would assuredly have been offensive; but one circumstance which completes the story, could have been thought of by none but Tintoret. The angel casts a shadow before him towards Adam and Eve.

RUSKIN

On the ceiling (restored, IFM), in the oval above the *Paradiso*, Veronese: *Apotheosis of Venice*

The matronly personification of Venice is shown enthroned in clouds (in which the supporting goddesses recline) in front of a vast arcade. On the balcony

On 3 October, 1786 Goethe sketched the lawyer Reccaini and wrote: 'In the Ducal Palace I witnessed an important trial. One of the advocates was everything an exaggerated 'buffo' should be: short and fat but agile, a very prominent profile, a booming voice and an impassioned eloquence as though everything he said came from the bottom of his heart.'

below, a group of ladies and gentlemen together with their children and pets, show a mild and aristocratic interest, and lower still two soldiers on charging stallions attempt to control the crowd . . . . The general effect of Veronese's painting is decidedly Baroque. Incompletely so, perhaps, for only in the lowest zone is there any real movement, while the whole lacks that display of emotion which was to be such an important element in infusing unity into the great decorative schemes of the succeeding century. Nevertheless, the elaborate illusionism of the architecture and the tremendous confidence and swagger of the conception produces an effect of momentarily stunning the senses which is altogether Baroque. And yet when we recover from the shock and bring ourselves to examine the work in detail, the ingredients are very much the same as in the classical Renaissance-like composition of the *Feast*[1] . . . . The figures have the same nobility and the same air of detachment. In principle, the *Triumph* is simply the *Feast* seen not at eye-level but from a great distance below.

If the seeming-Renaissance can be transformed so easily into the seeming-Baroque it is clear that the barriers between the two are less final than is usually supposed . . . . There was at this time no fundamental antagonism between the classical design of the Renaissance and the Baroque system . . . the former was the perfect vehicle of expression for placid subjects and the latter for animated ones.

GOULD

In the other oval
Palma Il Giovane: *Sovereign Venice being Crowned* (restored, I F M)

The frieze of ducal portraits has one missing (opposite the rostrum): it is that of Doge Marin Faliero.

Marino Faliero became Doge in 1354 when his age was seventy-six, having been both a soldier and a diplomatist. He found himself at once involved in the war with Genoa, and almost immediately came the battle of Sapienza, when the Genoese took five thousand prisoners, including the admiral, Niccoló Pisani. This blow was a very serious one for the Venetians, involving as it did great loss of life, and there was a growing feeling that they were badly governed. The Doge, who was but a figure-head of the Council of Ten, secretly thinking so too, plotted for the overthrow of the Council and the establishment of himself in

---

[1] Accademia, Room X, No.203 (p.82).

Avocato Reccaini

ad pag. 15.

supreme power. The Arsenal men were to form his chief army in the revolt; the false alarm of a Genoese attack was to get the populace together; and then the blow was to be struck and Faliero proclaimed prince. But the plot miscarried through one of the conspirators warning a friend to keep indoors; the ringleaders were caught and hanged or exiled; and the Doge, after confessing his guilt, was beheaded in the courtyard of his palace . . . Of his unhappy story Byron made a drama.

One of Faliero's party was Calendario, an architect, employed on the part of the Doge's Palace in which we are now standing. He was hanged or strangled between the two red columns in the upper arches of the Piazzetta façade. . .

Before leaving the Hall one should, as I have said, walk to the balcony, the door of which the custodian opens for each visitor with a mercenary hand. It should of course be free to all[1] and Venice would do well to appoint some official (if such could be found) to enforce such liberties. Immediately below is all the movements of the Molo; then the edge of the lagoon with its myriad gondolas; then the sparkling water, with all its busy activities and swaying gondoliers; and away beyond it the lovely island of S. Giorgio. A fairer prospect the earth cannot show.

LUCAS

The route returns through the Great Council Hall and leads over the Bridge of Sighs through part of the 'New' Prisons (built c16 and early c17) to the rooms of the Avogaria – a branch of the judiciary. In the second of these (the Notaries) there is a bookstall; in the Stanza della Bolla Ducale nearby (closed at time of writing)
Bombelli: *Portrait of Two Avogadori*

These full-lengths, which were to become so frequent and popular in 18th Century Venice, derive in the first place from the big votive paintings of the Renaissance, in which senators and doges solemnly kneel before an altar or a divine personage and in which they personify Venice. Everything in those pictures emphasized the hieratic; the grave profile and dignified gesture, the rich official clothes, all subduing the personality so that each man becomes only a symbol of the Republic itself.

But in the later work, the divine element has disappeared.

By the time of Bombelli's double portrait of the *Avogadori Pietro Garzoni and Francesco Benzon*, painted about 1683–84, we have only the undramatic Dove in the sky above the two men, one of whom rather shyly indicates its presence. The picture is frankly a double portrait, a vividly human one in which the celestial appurtenance is barely a distraction; and in other portraits of similar personages by Bombelli even this last faint intrusion is replaced by a plain setting about the figures.

LEVEY

---

[1] I found it so recently – MG.

One leaves via the prison cells.

About the air and light condition and the inhuman treatment meeted out to the prisoners in the *Pozzi*, many exaggerated accounts have been repeated especially by the democratic revolutionaries in 1797, or reported by not very scrupulous historians and writers, which resulted in exaggerated ideas of the terrifying and cruel methods of government of the ancient Republic. The Venetian administration, on the contrary, did not adopt more cruel methods than the other governments when all conditions and usages in those days are taken into account; indeed, it tried to alleviate the prisoners' lot with more humane treatment and with special improvements, and also by stimulating public charity. The 18 vaulted cells, built with blocks of Istrian stone, receive indirect light from the passage; they are divided into two rows and were covered with thick boards of wood; boards too served as beds; only one cell is today kept in its original state. Each cell used to have a special name (Galeotta, Vulcana, Moceniga, Leona), or was named with a Roman numeral upside down; on the walls, names, sentences and rough drawings, mostly of the c16, can still be seen.
LORENZETTI

I descended from the cheerful day into two ranges, one below another, of dismal, awful, horrible stone cells. They were quite dark. Each had a loophole in its massive walls, where, in the old time, every day a torch was placed, to light the prisoners within, for half an hour. The captives, by the glimmering of these brief rays, had cut and scratched inscriptions in the blackened vaults. I saw them. For their labour with the rusty nail's point had out-lived their agony and them through many generations.
    One cell I saw, in which no man remained for more than four-and-twenty hours, long marked for dead before he entered it. Hard by another, a dismal one, whereto, at midnight, the confessor came – a monk, brown-robed and hooded – ghastly in the day and free bright air, but in the midnight of the murky prison, Hope's extinguisher and Murder's herald. I had my foot upon the spot where, at the same dread hour, the shriven prisoner was strangled; and struck my hand upon the guilty door – low-browed and stealthy – through which the lumpish sack was carried out into a boat and rowed away, and drowned where it was death to cast a net.
DICKENS

The Council of Ten, which had a hand in everything, which disposed without appeal of life and death, of financial affairs and military appointments, which included the Inquisitors among its number, and which over-threw Foscari, as it had overthrown so many powerful men before – this Council was yearly chosen afresh from the whole governing body, the Gran Consiglio, and consequently was the most direct expression of its will. It is not probable that serious intrigues occurred at these elections, as the short duration of the office and the accountability which followed rendered it an object of no great desire. But violent and mysterious as the proceedings of this and other authorities might be, the genuine Venetian conoted rather than fled their sentence, not only because the Republic had long arms, and if it could not catch him, might punish his family, but because in most cases it acted from national motives, and not from a thirst

for blood. No State has ever exercised a greater moral influence over its subjects, whether abroad or at home. Every Venetian away from home was a born spy for his Government. It was a matter of course that the Venetian Cardinals at Rome sent home news of the transactions of secret Papal Consistories. Cardinal D. Grimani had the dispatches intercepted in the neighbourhood of Rome (1500) which Ascanio Sforza was sending to his brother Ludovico il Moro, and forwarded them to Venice; his father at that time exposed to a serious accusation claimed public credit for this service of his son before the Gran Consiglio.
BURCKHARDT

Correr Museum

We return to the Piazza. The entrance to the Correr Museum (open 10.00–16.00 weekdays; 9.00–12.30 Sunday; closed Tuesday) is under the colonnade at the end of the Piazza opposite to the Basilica.

In the sixth room, a number of stone fragments: on the left of the exit door a lion's mouth, used for secret accusations against tax evaders.

Two rooms further on
Heinz: *Processione Del Redentore*, showing the bridge of boats over to the Redentore church on the Giudecca.

The Picture Gallery (Quadreria) is at the far end and upstairs. The mounting of the pictures is striking, if a little self-conscious; but they are all clean, well hung and remarkably well lit.
    The following merit special attention:

Room 9
Two large paintings by Canaletto

Room 10
P. Breughel the Younger: *Adoration of the Magi*

Room 11
Bouts: *Madonna and Child*
da Messina: *Pieta*
van der Goes: *Crucifixion*

Prospetto della Piazza verso il Mare   F. Zucchi

For two generations the Zucchi family of artists and engravers portrayed the many aspects of Venice. This print was done early in C18 by Francesco Zucchi (1695–1764) whose son Andrea married the English artist Angelica Kaufman.

Room 12
Bruyn: *Portrait of a Woman*

Room 13
Jacopo Bellini: *Crucifixion*
Giovanni Bellini: *Madonna and Child*
Giovanni Bellini: *Pieta*

. . . the compositional scheme and the figure of Christ were taken from Donatello's bronze relief of the same subject, which was part of the high altar in the Santo,[1] while the angels were modelled on the music-making putti which in all probability once covered the plinths of the columns of the same altar.
WILDE

[1] In Padua.

Giovanni Bellini: *Transfiguration*

The picture which originally terminated in a cusped arch has been cut at the top, where we see the lower part of a red glory which probably originally contained the dove or a bust of the Father . . . Although it is not very large by the standard of Giovanni's later work this picture, which must have been originally nearly five feet high, is evidently a monumental altar painted for a church and not, like the other works we have considered, for private devotion, and the handling of the detail is correspondingly slightly coarser. It seems possible that it formed the central panel of a small polyptych and the accompanying panels might have given more evident relevance to the quotation from the Book of Job, MISEREMINI. MEI. SALTEM. VOS. AMICI. MEI., which appears on a large centrally placed *cartellino* at the foot of the panel, since its reference to the Transfiguration seems obscure. Perhaps, on the other hand, it is a prayer by the donor of the picture not directly relevant to its subject. . . .
ROBERTSON

Gentile Bellini: *Doge Giovanni Mocenigo*
Giovanni Bellini: *Crucifixion*

When one goes into the Renaissance galleries, it is as if one suddenly realized that in all the others one had been suffering from a blurred short-sightedness. And this is not because many of the paintings have been finely cleaned, nor because chiaroscuro was a later convention. It is because every Flemish and Italian Renaissance artist believed that it was his subject itself – not his way of painting it – which had to express the emotions and ideas he intended... . . It is this difference – the difference between the pictures being a starting-off point and a destination – that explains the clarity, the visual definitiveness, the tactile values of Renaissance art. The Renaissance painter limited himself to an exclusive concern with what the spectator could see, as opposed to what he might infer. . . .

This attitude had several important results. It forbade any attempt at literal naturalism because the only appeal of naturalism is the inference that it is 'just life like': it obviously isn't, in fact, like life because the picture is only a static image. It prevented all merely subjective suggestibility. It forced the artist, as far as his knowledge allowed him, to deal simultaneously with all the visual aspects of his subject – colour, light, mass, line, movement, structure, and not, as has increasingly happened since, to concentrate only on one aspect and to infer the others. It allowed him to combine more richly than any later artists have done realism and decoration, observation and formalization. The idea that they are incompatible is only based on today's assumption that their inferences are incompatible; visually an embroidered surface or drapery, invented as the most beautiful mobile architecture ever, can combine with realistic anatomical analysis as naturally as the courtly and physical combine in Shakespeare. But above all, the Renaissance artist's attitude made him use to its maximum the most expressive visual form in the world – the human body. Later the nude became an idea – Arcadia or Bohemia. But during the Renaissance every eyelid, breast, wrist, baby's foot, nostril, was a double celebration of fact: the fact of the miraculous structure of the human body and the fact that only through the senses of this body can we apprehend the rest of the visible, tangible world.

This lack of ambiguity is the Renaissance, and its superb combination of sensuousness and nobility stemmed from a confidence which cannot be artificially re-created. But when we eventually achieve a confident society again, its art may well have more to do with the Renaissance than with any of the moral or political artistic theories of the nineteenth century. Meanwhile, it is a salutary reminder for us even today that, as Berenson has said so often and so wisely, the vitality of European art lies in its 'tactile values and movement' which are the result of the observation of the 'corporal significance of objects'.
BERGER

Bellini's earliest known works . . . are still very Mantegna-like in feeling, but the outlines are already more pliant and the lighting subtler. In the *Crucifixion* of the Correr museum, the Virgin and Saint John still bear the mark of the Paduan painter's influence, but the vast landscape with its quiet river and golden horizon reveals a personal sense of luminous space. Giambellino gives increasing importance to the skies in his compositions and to the special quality of the atmosphere.
CHASTEL

Room 14
Alvise Vivarini: *Saint Anthony of Padua*
Compare with the figure in his *Sacred Conversation* – Accademia Gallery, Room XXII (p.93).

Room 15
Carpaccio: *Two Venetian Ladies*
The child and and the dog are cut off by the left-hand edge: the picture was formerly bigger. The roof terraces (Altane) are thought to provide an explanation for the 'golden tresses' of Venetian painting: the hair, wet with a chemical solution and spread over the brim of a crownless hat, bleached in the sun while giving shade to its owner.

I know . . . no other which unites every nameable quality of painter's art in so intense a degree – breadth with tenderness, brilliancy with quietness, decision with minuteness, colour with light and shade: all that is faithfullest in Holland, fancifullest in Venice, severest in Florence, naturalest in England. Whatever de Hooghe could do in shade, Van Eyck in detail, Giorgione in mass, Titian in colour, Bewick and Landseer in animal life, is here at once; and I know no other picture in the world which can be compared with it.
RUSKIN

It has been named 'The Two Courtesans', largely because of the daringly décolleté dresses. But these were in fact quite normal for bourgeois women in the 1490s, and the very high shoes are of a type worn only by the respectably married – 'those pattens must make it difficult for your wife to walk' remarked a traveller to a Venetian: 'so much the better' was the reply.

HONOUR

The growing delight in life with the consequent love of health, beauty, and joy were felt more powerfully in Venice than anywhere else in Italy. The explanation of this may be found in the character of the Venetian government which was such that it gave little room for the satisfaction of the passion for personal glory, and kept its citizens so busy in duties of state that they had small leisure for learning. Some of the chief passions of the Renaissance thus finding no outlet in Venice, the other passions insisted all the more on being satisfied. Venice, moreover, was the only state in Italy which was enjoying, and for many generations had been enjoying, internal peace. This gave the Venetians a love of comfort, of ease and of splendour, a refinement of manner, and humaneness of feeling, which made them the first really modern people in Europe.

Thus it came to pass that in the Venetian pictures of the end of the fifteenth century we find neither the contrition nor the devotion of those earlier years when the Church alone employed painting as the interpreter of emotions, nor the learning which characterised the Florentines. The Venetian masters of this time, although nominally continuing to paint the Madonna and saints, were in reality painting handsome, healthy, sane people like themselves, people who wore their splendid robes with dignity, who found life worth the mere living and sought no metaphysical basis for it.

The Church itself had educated its children to understanding painting as a language. Now that the passions men dared to avow were no longer connected with happiness in some future state only, but mainly with life in the present, painting was expected to give voice to these more human aspirations and to desert the outgrown ideals of the Church.

BERENSON

Room 16
Carpaccio: *Man in a Red Hat*

Room 17
Lotto: *Madonna and Child Crowned with Angels*
See also Riccio's bust in this room.

While staying in Venice in the years 1495–96 Dürer made a series of studies of Venetians. These two drawings from the Tarocchi series are of an aristocrat with his page, and of the Doge Augustino Barbarigo.

Once did she hold the gorgeous East in fee,
And was the safeguard of the West: the worth
Of Venice did not fall below her birth,
Venice, the eldest child of liberty.
She was a maiden city, bright and free;
No guile seduced, no force could violate;
And when she took unto herself a mate,
She must espouse the everlasting sea.
And what if she had seen those glories fade,
Those titles vanish, and that strength decay,
Yet shall some tribute of regret be paid
When her long life hath reached its final day:
Men are we, and must grieve when even the shade
Of that which once was great has passed away.
WORDSWORTH

Walk 2

Santa Maria della Salute – Accademia – Peggy Guggenheim Collection

This walk begins at the vaporetto station Salute. This is on the route of line No.1. Alternatively, it may be reached from the Piazza by taking the exit in the sw corner. Follow the way ahead, cross two canals and reach Campo Santa Maria del Giglio. Turn left and take the traghetto to the opposite side of the Canal. Continue down the Calle del Tragheto, take the first turn to the left, pass through Campo San Gregorio and emerge beside the Salute church.

Further down the Canal is the customs house (Dogana). On the tower at one end, a revolving statue of Fortune, standing on a gilded sphere (restored, Banco San Marco), supported by two Atlantes.

The statue of Fortune, forming the weathercock, standing on the world, is alike characteristic of the conceits of the time and of the hopes and principles of the last days of Venice.
RUSKIN

The charming architectural promontory of the Dogana stretches out the most graceful arms, balancing in its hand the gilded globe on which revolves the delightful satirical figure of a little weathercock of a woman. This Fortune, this Navigation, or whatever she is called – she surely needs no name – catches the wind in a bit of drapery of which she has divested her rotary bronze loveliness. On the other side of the Canal twinkles and glitters the long row of the happy palaces which are mainly expensive hotels. There is a little of everything everywhere, in the bright Venetian air, but to these houses belongs especially the appearance of sitting, across the water, at the receipt of custom, of watching in their hypocritical loveliness for the stranger and the victim. I call them happy because even their sordid uses and their vulgar signs melt somehow, with their vague sea-stained pinks and drabs, into that strange gaiety of light and colour which is made up of the reflection of superannuated things. The atmosphere plays over them like a laugh, they are of the essence of places as they are from their own balconies, and share fully in that universal privilege of Venetian objects which consists of being both the picture and the point of view.
HENRY JAMES

Santa Maria della Salute

The church of Santa Maria della Salute (open **8.00–12.00**; **15.00–18.00**) – 'of health' – was built to celebrate the end of a plague in the c17.

In **1630** the Senate voted funds for the building of Santa Maria della Salute. Longhena's design was accepted a year later and Marco Boschini made the engraving (opposite) from Longhena's model to show how the opening ceremony might look. The building was completed in **1681** and consecrated in **1687**.

Venice is nowadays unthinkable without the picturesque silhouette of the church, which dominates the entrance to the Canal Grande; but it would be wrong to insist too much on the picturesqueness of the building, as is usually done, while forgetting that this is in every respect one of the most interesting and subtle structures of the entire 17th century.
The salient feature of the plan is a regular octagon surrounded by an ambulatory. . . . The elevation . . . is a free adaptation of a well-known North Italian type derived from Bramante, Santa Maria della Salute differing from the Renaissance models mainly in the decorative interpretation of the columns. Instead of continuing the columns of the octagon into the architecture of the drum, we find a large figure topping the projecting entablature of each column. It is these iconographically important figures of prophets that turn each column into an isolated unit and at the same time emphasise the enclosed centralised character of the main room. . . .

From Palladio derives the colouristic treatment: grey stone for the structural parts and whitewash for the walls and fillings. But it should be remembered that this was not Palladio's speciality: it had, in fact, a mediaeval pedigree, was taken up and systemised by Brunelleschi, and after him used by most architects who were connected with the classical Florentine tradition. The architects of the Roman Baroque never employed this method of differentiation, the isolating effect of which would have interfered with the dynamic rhythms of their buildings. In contrast, however, to Florentine procedure, where colour invariably sustains a coherent metrical system, Longhena's colour scheme is not logical; colour for him was an optical device which enabled him to support or suppress elements of the composition, thereby directing the beholder's vision.

Many details of the Salute are also Palladian, such as the orders, the columns placed on high pedestals (see S. Giorgio Maggiore) and the segmental windows with mullions in the chapels, the type derived from Roman thermae and introduced by Palladio into ecclesiastical architecture (S. Giorgio, Il Redentore). All these elements combine to give the Salute the severe and chaste appearance of a Palladian structure, but it can be shown that Palladio's influence was even more vital.

WITTKOWER

Let us now enter the church.

Marco Boschini: Santa Maria della Salute (from the 'Gran Teatro di Venezia', 1720).

One of Longhena's chief problems consisted in preserving the octagonal form outside without sacrificing clarity and lucidity inside. By the seemingly simple device of making the sides of two consecutive pillars parallel to each other he succeeded in giving the optically important units of the ambulatory and the chapels regular geometrical shapes, entirely in the spirit of the Renaissance. The full meaning of this organisation is revealed only when one stands in the ideal and real centre of the octagon. Looking from this point in any direction, the spectator will find that entirely homogeneous 'pictures' always appear in the field of vision. Longhena's passionate interest in determining the holder's field of vision is surely one of the factors which made him choose the problematical octagon with ambulatory instead of one of the traditional Renaissance designs over a centralised plan. It cannot be emphasised too strongly that no other type of plan allows only carefully integrated views to be seen; here the eye is not given a chance to wander off and make conquests of its own.

It would seem that the centralisation of the octagon could not have been carried any further. Moreover, the sanctuary which is reached over a few steps, appears only loosely connected with the octagon. Following the North Italian Renaissance tradition of centralised plans (Bramante's Santa Maria di Canepanova), main room and sanctuary form almost independent units. For the two large apses of the domed sanctuary Longhena employed a system entirely different from that of the octagon; he used giant pilasters instead of columns and replaced the mullioned windows of the chapel by normal windows in two tiers. . . .

A third room, the rectangular choir, is separated from the sanctuary by an arch resting on pairs of free-standing columns, between which the view is blocked by the large High Altar. Inside the choir the architecture changes again: two small orders of pilasters are placed one above the other. At the far end of the choir three small arches appear in the field of vision.

From the entrance of the church the columns and the arch framing the High Altar lie in the field of vision – it is important that only this motif and no more is visible – and the beholder is directed to the spiritual centre of the church through a sequence of arches, one behind the other: from the octagon to the ambulatory and the altar and, concluding the vista, to the arched wall of the choir. Thus, in spite of the Renaissance-like isolation of spatial entities and in spite of the carefully calculated centralisation of the octagon, there is a scenic progression along the longitudinal axis. . . .

In Santa Maria della Salute scenery appears behind scenery like wings on the stage. Instead of inviting the eye – as the Roman Baroque architects did – to glide along the walls and savour a spatial continuum, Longhena constantly determines the vistas across the spaces. . . .

WITTKOWER

The fabric of the church has been extensively restored by the Comité français pour la sauvegarde de Venise.

In the sacristy (entrance slightly to left of high altar), on the wall opposite the entrance
Basaiti (attr.): *St Sebastian*

To the left of *St Sebastian*
Tintoretto: *Marriage at Cana*

. . . one is surprised to find Tintoret whose tone of mind was always grave, and
who did not like to make a picture out of brocades and diadems, throwing his
whole strength into the conception of a marriage feast; but so it is, and there are
assuredly no female heads in any of his pictures in Venice elaborated so far as
those which here form the central light. Neither is it often that the works of this
mighty master conform themselves to any of the rules acted upon by ordinary
painters; but in this instance the popular laws have been observed, and an
academy student would be delighted to see with what severity the principal
light is arranged in a central mass, which is divided and made more brilliant by
a vigorous piece of shadow thrust into the midst of it, and which dies away in
lesser fragments and sparkling towards the extremities of the picture. This mass
of light is as interesting by its composition as by its intensity. The cicerone who
escorts the stranger round the sacristy in the course of five minutes, which allows
him some forty seconds for the contemplation of a picture, which the study of
six months would not entirely fathom, directs his attention very carefully to the
'bell' effetto di prospettiva', the whole merit of the picture being, in the eyes of
the intelligent public, that there is a long table in it, one end of which looks
farther off than the other; but there is more in the 'bell' effetto di prospettivo'
than the observance of the common law of optics. The table is set in a spacious
chamber, of which the windows at the end let in the light from the horizon, and
those in the side wall the intense blue of an Eastern sky. The spectator looks all
along the table, at the farther end of which are seated Christ, and the Madonna,
the marriage guests on each side of it – on one side men, on the other women;
the men are set with their backs to the light, which passing over their heads and
glancing slightly on the tablecloth, falls in full length along the line of young
Venetian women, who thus fill the whole centre of the picture with one broad
sunbeam, made up of fair faces and golden hair. Close to the spectator a woman
has risen in amazement, and stretches across the table to show the wine in her
cup to those opposite; her dark red dress intercepts and enhances the mass of
gathered light. It is rather curious, considering the subject of the picture, that
one cannot distinguish either the bride or bridegroom; but the fourth figure from
the Madonna in the line of women, who wears a white head-dress of lace and
rich chains of pearls in her hair, may well be accepted for the former, and I think
that between her and the woman on the Madonna's left hand the unity of the
line of women is intercepted by a male figure. The tone of the whole picture is
sober and majestic in the highest degree; the dresses are all broad masses of
colour, and the only parts of the picture which lay claim to the expression of
wealth or splendour are the head-dresses of the women. In this respect the
conception of the scene differs widely from that of Veronese, and approaches more
nearly to the probable truth. Still the marriage is not an unimportant one; an
immense crowd, filling the background, forming a superbly rich mosaic of colour
against the distant sky. Taken as a whole, the picture is perhaps the most
perfect example which human art has produced of the utmost possible force and
sharpness of shadow united with richness of local colour. This picture unites
colour as rich as Titian's with light and shade as forcible as Rembrandt's, and
far more decisive.
RUSKIN

Over altar

Titian: *Five Saints*

An early work (1508–9), probably commissioned in response to an outbreak of the plague: St Mark's face and arm are cast into gloom by the shadow from the pillars on the right, and around him are gathered the saints traditionally invoked against the plague – Cosmas and Damian, Roch and Sebastian.

> . . . the principal figure is an impressive silhouette against the sky. Actually there are two viewpoints, and the figure of St. Mark, seated on his throne like a Roman emperor, appears more foreshortened than it ought to be, but this foreshortening connects it more closely with the plastic groups below.
> WILDE

Altar front

c15 tapestry: *Descent of Holy Ghost*

On ceiling three panels by Titian: *The Sacrifice of Abraham, David Killing Goliath, Cain and Abel*

We return to the church and follow the ambulatory to the left until we reach the last chapel before the main door. On the altar.

Giordano: *Presentation of the Virgin*

> The great building of seventeenth century Venice – the sole great artistic feat of the city in that century – was Longhena's S. Maria della Salute; and it is hardly an exaggeration to say that this church with its air-borne domes and sea-washed steps needed merely to be brushed on to the canvasses of Canaletto and Guardi to become rococo.
> Rococo before its time, it was suitably decorated by a non-Venetian painter, rococo also before the time, Luca Giordano (1632–1705). He left three altarpieces in the church, of which the *Presentation of the Virgin* with its elaborate architectural setting and its radiant shafts of light preludes the new style and also provides a welcome piece of grand decoration amid the gloomy darkness of seventeenth century Venetian art. Despite its grimy appearance today, the picture is really painted with startlingly bright cool colours: there is generous use of white and a strong blue juxtaposed to it – very much as Tiepolo was to juxtapose them half a century later in the Palazzo Labia frescoes. The commission for these altar pieces was given to Giordano in 1685 and reveals that the visiting artist was preferred for this important work to any native talent available at the time. Giordano's legacy to Venice did not go unperceived, it seems, and a few years later the style of his altarpieces was no longer an isolated phenomenon but, made more graceful and less rigorous, had become a Venetian style.
> LEVEY

We leave the church and look back at the façade.

Like the interior, the picturesque exterior of Santa Maria della Salute was the result of sober deliberation. The thrust of the large dome is diverted onto pairs of buttresses (the Scrolls) which rest on the arches of the ambulatory. The side walls of the chapels (aligned with these arches) are therefore buttments to the dome. . . .

The large dome of the Salute has an inner and outer vault, the outer one consisting of lead over wood, in keeping with the Venetian custom (including Palladio). While the principal dome ultimately derives from that of St. Peter's, the subsiduary dome with its stilted form over a simple circular brick drum and framed by two campanili follows the Byzantine-Venetian tradition. The grouping together of a main and subsidiary dome fits well into the Venetian *ambiente* – the domes of S. Marco are quite near – but never before has the silhouette been so boldly enriched by the use of entirely different types of domes and drums in one and the same building. No less important than the aspect of the domes from a distance is the near view of the lower zone from the Canal Grande. From here the chapels right and left of the main entrance are conspicuous. They are therefore elaborately treated like little church façades in their own right. . . . Their small order is taken up in the gigantic triumphal arch motif in the main entrance. It is this motif that sets the seal on the entire composition.

The central arch with the framing columns corresponds exactly to the interior arches of the octagon, so that the theme is given before one enters the church. In addition the small order also repeats that inside, and the niches for statues in two tiers conform to the windows in the sanctuary. And more than this: the façade is, in fact, devised like a *scenae frons*, and with the central door thrown wide open, as shown in a contemporary engraving, the consequitive sequence of arches inside the church contained by the triumphal arch, conjures up a proper stage setting.

WITTKOWER

From the church we take the bridge over the water-way (Ponte dell'Abbazia di San Gregorio) and go on, via Campo San Gregorio and Calle San Gregorio (glass blowing at No. 175b) to the Campo Barbaro, then over the Ponte San Cristofolo past the entrance to the Peggy Guggenheim Collection (described on p.94) to Campo San Vio. Immediately to the right on entering we see the English Church.

. . . For a taste of Venetian Englishry, go on a summer morning to the Anglican Church of St. George, which is a converted warehouse near the Accademia bridge. Its pews are usually full, and the familiar melodies of Ancient and Modern stream away, turgid but enthusiastic, across the Grand Canal. The drone of the visiting padre blends easily with the hot buzz of the Venetian summer, and when the service ends you will see his surplice fluttering in the doorway, among the neat hats and tweedy suits, the white gloves and prayer-books, the scrubbed children and the pink-cheeked, tight-curled, lavender-scented, pearl-necklaced regimentally brooched ladies that so admirably represent year in, year out, east and west, the perennial spirit of England abroad.

Nowadays they are only summer visitors, and in winter the little church is
closed, and looks neglected and forgotten. Once, though, it was the flourishing
chapel of the permanent Anglo-American community in Venice, in the days
when there was such a thing. Around its walls are elegant epitaphs to forgotten
English gentlewomen, often titled and usually the daughters of gallant officers;
and sometimes you will find upon your seat a curiously anachronistic appeal for
funds, which was evidently overprinted when it first appeared half a century
ago, and is still faithfully distributed – although the chaplain, the British and
American Hospital and the Seamen's Institute for which it appeals have all long
since disappeared.
MORRIS

It is worth going down to the water for the view across the Canal, and
especially for the view of the large palazzo opposite and a little to the
right – Sansovino's Palazzo Corner della Ca'Grande, a c16 building with a
profound influence on c17 palaces.

The classical elements, rusticated on the ground floor, Ionic and Corinthian on
the first and second, are adapted to the constructional character of the city and
to the traditional Venetian house in which the windows and ample terraces in
the forms of loggias acquire fundamental importance in the architectural
mass because of the prevalence of empty spaces over solid ones.
LORENZETTI

Over the bridge out of the campo, and on the right is the Cini Museum
(not open at the time of writing).

After visiting the museum, return to the Campo San Vio, turn right
along the Fondamenta di Ca'Bragadin, and emerge facing the Giudecca
Island across the Giudecca Canal.

On the opposite side of the water is Palladio's church of the Redentore
(see illustration, opposite).

Turn right over the bridge and along the Fondamenta delle Zattere to
the c18 church of the Gesuati (restored, Stifterverband für die Deutsche
Wissenschaft and the Comité français pour la sauvegarde de Venise).

---

*Giuseppe Valeriani drew the Redentore (upper drawing) as he saw it in 1719
when he first arrived in Venice, and one hundred years later Turner sketched
Palladio's other water-side church, San Giorgio (below). The façade of San
Giorgio was completed by Vincenzo Scamozzi (1552–1616) between 1597
and 1610. Palladio's original designs called for the pillars and pilasters to
begin at the same level, as in the façade of the Redentore. The pillars and
pilasters of his other church façade – that of San Francesco della Vigna
(p.101) – also have a uniform base but are raised off the ground by a plinth.
Scamozzi appears to have combined these two features with a not altogether
happy result.*

On the ceiling
Three frescoes by G. B. Tiepolo
These are early works, remarkable for their delicate coloration and dramatic foreshortening. In the central panel, St Dominic distributes rosaries to the crowd, the Virgin appearing overhead.

Right side, first chapel
G. B. Tiepolo: *Virgin and Saints*

Right side, third chapel
Piazzetta: *Three Saints*

While colour was brightening even garishly the rococo painter's canvases, Piazzetta was restricting his palette to chestnut, black white and grey. Working within that deliberately narrow range, his genius achieved at least one great tonal coup in *Saints Vincent Hyacinth and Lorenzo Bertrando* for the new Dominican church, the Gesuati: an altarpiece which is probably the greatest picture of its kind set up in Venice in the 18th century. He simply disposes his three saints in a cloudy nondescript atmosphere and from their juxtaposed habits of black, white and grey, he makes more effective contrast than would another painter with a whole rainbow of colours. Unlike the majority of his contemporaries he aims at tonal effects, gradations and harmonies of monochrome, and he cuts down the amount of light in the picture in a manner almost rebuking the superb chromatic brilliance of Tiepolo's ceiling in the same church, also painted in 1739.

The taste for reproducing the trivia of life which runs in Venice from the history painters, to the view painters, via genre, is absent from Piazzetta. The clothes of his people have a simplicity that is sculptural; and his concentration on the figure, like his subdued unified tonality, is sculptural too. Perhaps there is really some genuine relevance in the fact that his father had been a sculptor or a wood-carver; perhaps from him Piazzetta inherited that feeling for the monumental that makes him stand out so boldly and forcefully amid the gentle coloured mists of most 18th century Venetian art.
LEVEY

Left side, first chapel (i.e. last before exit)
Sebastiano Ricci: *Pius V and Saints*

Turn right outside the church. There is a 'Lion's Mouth' let into the wall at No.919. Like the others, it was used for anonymous accusations – in this case concerning the sanitary department.

Continue along the Fondamenta and turn right just before the bridge. On the opposite side of the water we see the last remaining *squero* – where gondolas are built and repaired. The white church, with large thermal windows, is San Trovaso. Continue along this Fondamenta as far as possible, then turn right, to emerge in the Campo de la Carità.

The entrance to the Academy (open 9.00–14.00 weekdays; 9.30–13.00 Sunday; closed Monday) is on the right. Just beyond the foot of the Accademia Bridge is a spot for coffee. The wooden bridge was built in 1932, replacing the iron bridge – the 'Ponte Inglese' of 1854.

As late as 1848 the Austrian soldiers could prevent subversive foot passage across the city simply by closing the Rialto bridge. Then two iron structures were thrown across the water-way – one by the railway station, one near the Accademia gallery. They were flat, heavy, and very ugly, and the Accademia bridge was sometimes known, in mixed irony and affection, as *Ponte Inglese*. Both lasted until the 1930s, when they had to be replaced because of the increased size of the 'vaporetti'. The new station bridge was a handsome stone structure, far higher than the Rialto. The new Accademia bridge was of precisely the same proportions, but because money was short it was built (just for the time being, so they cheerfully said) of tarred wood – a return to the original materials of Venetian bridge building.
MORRIS

My tendency to look at the world through the eyes of the painter whose pictures I have seen last has given me an odd idea. Since our eyes are educated from childhood on by the objects we see around us, a Venetian painter is bound to see the world as a brighter and gayer place than most people see it. We northerners who spend our lives in a drab and, because of the dirt and dust, an uglier country where even reflected light is subdued, and who have, most of us, to live in cramped rooms – we cannot instinctively develop an eye which looks with such delight at the world.

As I glided over the lagoons in the brilliant sunshine and saw the gondoliers in their colourful costume, gracefully poised against the blue sky as they rowed with easy strokes across the light-green surface of the water, I felt I was looking at the latest and best painting of the Venetian school. The sunshine raised the local colours to a dazzling glare and even the parts in shadow were so light that they could have served pretty well as sources of light. The same could be said of the reflections in the water. Everything was painted clearly on a clear background. It only needed the sparkle of a white-crested wave to put the dot on the i.
GOETHE

Accademia

Room I
facing entrance
No.21: Paolo Veneziano: *Coronation of the Virgin*
The composite altarpiece – which Paolo played his part in popularizing –
brought the Byzantine mosaic figures down to human level and scale and
became the most important element in Venetian church decoration from
c14 to c16. A c14 church in Venice (see San Zanipolo p.120 and Frari,
p.141) was not decorated with fresco cycles, as it might be in Tuscany or
Padua; it was decorated with individual works – the thin, olive-skinned,
gentle saints of Byzantium set in the brilliant blue and gilding of a
polyptich like this, standing out in the soft light of the Gothic windows.

The first name to appear in the history of Venetian painting is that of Paolo
Veneziano, who worked between 1321 and 1360. His manner is closely related to
the Byzantine art of the period, with which he may have become familiar
during a visit to Constantinople, or simply through the numerous mosaics,
icons and miniatures in Venice. However he gradually acquired a more supple
style, closer to the elegance of the Italian Trecento.

At the time he was painting the *Coronation of the Virgin* (ca. 1345) he was still
wavering between these two forms of expression. The motifs in the *Coronation
of the Virgin* derive from the 13th century Greek miniatures, the figures of
Saints have the same delicacy, the gold-embroidered gowns and Santa Clara's
striped cloak are of Oriental fabrics. But iconographic details, such as the
Virgin's crown and the angels holding the draperies behind the central group,
belong to the Gothic tradition. The sharper brush-strokes and the freer
arrangement of draperies further indicate a development that culminated in his
late works: the *Madonna* in the Louvre (1353) and the *Coronation of the Virgin*
in the Frick Collection (1358).

Thus even though he remained unaware of Giotto's decisive contribution,
Paolo Veneziano's art bears the mark of Western elegance. By remaining
faithful to the bright colours and gold ornamentation of Byzantine splendour,
Paolo determined the precious, decorative manner of late 14th century art.
CHASTEL

Room II
No.36: Cima da Conegliano: *Madonna and Saints*
No.166: Giovanni Bellini: *Mourning for Jesus*
No.611: Cima da Conegliano: *St Thomas*
No.44: Carpaccio: *Presentation of Jesus in the Temple*
No.815: Cima da Conegliano: *Madonna of the Orange-Tree*
No.39: Marco Basaiti: *Calling of the Sons of Zebedee*
No.38: Giovanni Bellini: *Madonna and Saints* (cf. Frari Triptych – p.141)

Such paintings are known as 'Sacre Conversazioni', because of their rapt stillness of mood, in which the Saints, scarcely looking at one another, seem to communicate at a spiritual rather than at a material level. Bellini's second 'Sacra Conversazione' is the San Giobbe altarpiece, painted for the church of that name, but now in the Accademia. This, unlike the others was painted for a Renaissance church so that the forms of its classically conceived architecture could be a direct continuation, suitably enriched, of those of the church itself. The viewpoint was so calculated that when the painting was *in situ* the figures seemed to be seen from the eye-level of the average spectator, and the chapel in the painting really seemed to open off the church.
STEER

No.69: Marco Basaiti: *Agony in the Garden.*

Its inspiration is obviously Bellinesque, and although the theme derives from the Bellini of half a century earlier, the breadth of the handling owes something to later works of the master. The glow of the sky round the figure of Christ is altogether in the spirit of Bellini, but the conception of the scene – as of a proscenium arch with the curtain up and the four saints standing like a chorus outside it – strikes, in an easel picture, a somewhat artificial and un-Bellinesque note. At the same time it has a certain effectiveness as decoration.
GOULD

What is it that makes these so fundamentally different from nearly all the works – and especially our own – that have followed them? The question may seem naïve. Social and stylistic historians, economists, chemists and psychologists have spent their lives defining and explaining this and many other differences between individual artists, periods, and whole cultures. Such research is invaluable, but its complexity often hides from us two simple, very obvious facts. The first is that it is our own culture, not foreign ones, which can teach us the keenest lessons: the culture of individualist humanism which began in Italy in the thirteenth century. And the second fact is that, at least in painting, a fundamental break occurred in this culture two and a half centuries after it began. After the sixteenth century artists were more psychologically profound (Rembrandt), more successfully ambitious (Rubens), more evocative (Claude); but they also lost an ease and a visual directness which precluded all pretentions; they lost what Berenson called 'tactile values'. After 1600 the great artists, pushed by lonely compulsion, stretch and extend the range of painting, break down its frontiers. Watteau breaks out towards music, Goya towards the stage, Picasso towards pantomime. A few such as Chardin, Corot, Cézanne, did accept the strictest limitations. But before 1550 every artist did. One of the most important results of this difference is that in the great later forays only genius could triumph: before even a small talent could give profound pleasure.
BERGER

No.89: Carpaccio: *Crucifixion on Mt. Ararat.*

Room III
No.102: Basaiti: *Saint George and Dragon*

Rooms IV and V
No.588: Mantegna: *Saint George*
No.47: Piero della Francesca: *Saint Jerome*
No.628: Cosmè Tura: *Madonna and Child*
No.613: Giovanni Bellini: *Madonna, Saint Catherine and the Magdalen*
No.586: Memling: *Portrait of a Youth*
No.610: Giovanni Bellini: *Madonna, Saint Paul and Saint George*
No.881: Giovanni Bellini: *Madonna and Child, between the Baptist and a saint*
No.883: Giovanni Bellini: *Pietà*
(Views of monuments in Vicenza are incorporated in the background)
No.612: Giovanni Bellini *Madonna of the Red Cherubs*
No.596: Giovanni Bellini: *Madonna of the Little Trees*
No.594: Giovanni Bellini: *Madonna and Child in a landscape*
No.595: Giovanni Beillini: *Allegorical Panels*
Bellini's five small allegorical panels were painted about 1490 for the frame of an elaborate mirror.

> In the most recent study of his work, Edgar Wind interprets them as a contrast between virtuous love (*Fortuna Amoris*) and its reward (*Cornes Virtutis*) on the one hand and, on the other, anguish (*Servitudo Acediae*) and vain illusions (*Vana Gloria*), the consequence of sinful love, represented by a woman holding a mirror. The four figures are accompanied by a blind harpy representing *Nemesis* (Revenge). These learned allusions, which recur in the 16th century books of emblems, were perhaps chosen to suggest the good and bad uses that can be made of a mirror.
> CHASTEL

No.915: Giorgione: *The Tempest.*

> The Venetian had as a rule very little personal religion, and consequently did not care for pictures that moved him to contrition or devotion. He preferred to have some pleasantly coloured thing that would put him into a mood connected with the side of life he most enjoyed – with refined merrymaking, with country parties, or with the sweet dreams of youth. Venetian painting alone among Italian schools was ready to satisfy such a demand, and it thus became the first genuinely modern art: for the most vital difference that can be indicated between the arts in antiquity and modern times is this; that now the arts tend to address themselves more and more to the actual needs of men, while in olden times they were supposed to serve some more than human purpose.
>   The pictures required for a house were naturally of a different kind for those suited to the Council Hall or the School, where large paintings, which could be

filled with many figures, were in place. For the house smaller pictures were necessary, such as could easily be carried about. The mere dimensions, therefore, excluded pageants but, in any case, the pageant was too formal a subject to suit all moods – too much like a brass band always playing in the room. The easel picture had to be without too definite a subject, and could no more permit being translated into words than a sonata.

Giorgione combined the fine feeling and poetry of Bellini with Carpaccio's gaiety and love of beauty and colour. Stirred with the enthusiasms of his own generation as people who have lived through other phases of feeling could not be, Giorgione painted pictures so perfectly in touch with the ripened spirit of the Renaissance that they met with the success which those things only find that at the same moment wake us to the full sense of a need and satisfy it.

Giorgione's life was short and very few of his works – not a score in all – have escaped destruction. But these suffice to give us a glimpse into that brief moment when the Renaissance found its most genuine expression in painting.

Our real interest in Italian painting is at botton an interest in that art which we almost instinctively feel to have been the fittest expression found by a period in that history of modern Europe which has much in common with youth. The Renaissance has the fascination of those years when we seemed so full of promise both with ourselves and to everybody else.

BERENSON

The small picture known as the *Tempest* – which is one of only two or three whose attribution to Giorgione has never been doubted and which on the strength of an inscription on the back of a comparable painting now at Vienna probably dates from around 1506 – is the quintessence of the Giorgionesque. For centuries its subject defeated all who tried to read a meaning into it, but X-rays have recently shown that there was originally a further female form in the place now occupied by the young man and for this reason (since two such different characters could hardly be interchangeable) it seems most logical to assume that no specific 'story' is being told and that the whole is a fantasy. Such, indeed, is its mood. Nothing like it has been painted before, and its strangeness and unearthly beauty is still potent after four centuries. The naked woman suckling her child, half watched by the (fully dressed) young man standing impassively as if on guard, a pair of broken columns (with an extra brick at the base of their plinth merely for pictorial reasons), part of an improbable building on the left, the bridge over the torrent (which may or may not be continuous with the water in the foreground: we have no means of deciding), more buildings (including one with an oriental dome) in the background, and a stormy sky overhead – the whole thing has the fantastic inconsequence of a dream, and this may, indeed, provide some clue to its origin. For not long before, in 1499, a curious romance, the *Hypnerotomachia Poliphili*, had been published at Venice and widely read. In this the conduct of all human affairs is likened to a dream, and a dream-like quality informs much of its narrative. One of its plates shows ruined columns as in the Tempest, and although the painting can hardly be regarded as an actual illustration of the book it may well be that Giorgione had had the Hypnerotomachia in mind shortly before painting this extraordinary and beautiful work.

GOULD

One day the episode here illustrated may be identified – the story, perhaps, of a
mother of some future hero, who was cast out of the city into the wilderness with
her child and was there discovered by a friendly young shepherd. For this, it
seems, is what Giorgione wanted to represent. But it is not due to its content that
the picture is one of the most wonderful things in art. Though the figures are not
particularly carefully drawn, and though the composition is somewhat artless,
the picture is clearly blended into a whole simply by the light and air that
permeates it all. It is the weird light of a thunderstorm and for the first time, it
seems, the landscape before which the actors of the picture move is not just a
background. It is there, by its own right, as the real subject of the painting. We
look from the figures to the scenery which fills the major part of the small
panel, and then back again, and we feel somehow that unlike his predecessors and
contemporaries; Giorgione has not drawn things and persons to arrange them
afterwards in space, but that he really thought of nature, the earth, the trees,
the light, air and clouds and the human beings with their cities and bridges as
one. In a way, this was almost as big a step forward into a new realm as the
invention of perspective had been. From now on, painting was more than
drawing plus colouring. It was an art with its own secret laws and devices.
GOMBRICH

No.272: Giorgione: *Old Woman*

The Portrait of an Old Woman in the Academy, generally attributed to him,
displays a startling realism and an attention to detail rather far removed from
Giorgione's usual manner and reminiscent of Northern painting.
CHASTEL

I feel tempted to let my fancy run free, and to weave the plot of a romance around
these two pictures, the *Soldier and Gypsy* or *Tempesta* and the *Old Woman*
'*Col Tempo*'. The soldier would be the young Giorgione himself looking on while
the somewhat more mature woman was giving suck to his and her child. She
may be suffering a revulsion of feeling against him for having brought her to
this pass, and he painted her as she would look when old, as an admonition to
gather roses while she might for time was aflying.
BERENSON

Room VI
No.291: Bonifacio: *Dives and Lazurus*

The elegant figures in the vestibule of a beautiful c16 Venetian villa are
contrasted with the figure of the begger in the foreground, and seem
unaware of the conflagration in the background: the subject matter does
little more than offer the occasion for this painter's virtuoso handling of
colour and light.

Room VII
No.912: Lorenzo Lotto: *Portrait of a Young Man in his Study*

Toward the middle of the sixteenth century, when elsewhere in Italy painting was trying to adapt itself to the hypocrisy of a Church whose chief reason for surviving as an institution was that it helped Spain to subject the world to tyranny, and when portraits were already exhibiting the fascinating youths of an earlier generation turned into obsequious and elegant courtiers – in Venice painting kept true to the ripened and more reflective spirit which succeeded to the most glowing decades of the Renaissance. This led men to take themselves more seriously, to act with more consideration of consequences, and to think of life with less hope and exultation. Quieter joys were sought, the pleasures of friendship and of the affections. Life not having proved the endless holiday it had promised to be, earnest people began to question whether under the gross masque of the official religion there was not something to console them for departed youth and for the failure of hopes. Thus religion began to revive in Italy, this time not ethnic nor political, but personal – an answer to the real needs of the human soul.

It is scarcely to be wondered at that the Venetian artist in whom we first find the expression of the new feelings, should have been one who by wide travel had been brought in contact with the miseries of Italy in a way not possible for those who had remained sheltered in Venice. Lorenzo Lotto, when he is most himself, does not paint the triumph of man over his environment, but in his altar pieces, and even more in his portraits, he shows us people in want of the consolation of religion, of sober thought, of friendship and affection. They look out from his canvasses as if begging for sympathy.

BERENSON

Titian and Tintoretto represent their sitters erect, stately and at their best or better than their best, as what they wanted to be taken for rather than as what, in their hearts, they knew themselves to be. In other words, Titian and Tintoretto painted ceremonial portraits and, but for the grace of genius, anticipated the effigies still perpetrated annually in the Royal Academy of London. Not so *Lotto*. Already in his earliest portraits *Lotto* could portray individuals, not mere types: individuals with personal preoccupations and feelings, and with moods of their own. Through a career of 60 years he was always painting what was most peculiarly characteristic in the sitter at the moment he was portraying him. Psychological snapshots? Yes, if you like, but serious, grave even, and stylized by art and never common, let alone vulgar, as in the performances of some of his Northern contemporaries. Scarcely any other artist can offer the variety of types that we discover in the portraits of *Lorenzo Lotto*. It almost would seem as if he had acquired the reputation of being the artist able to portray the kind of individual, who for personal, social or financial reasons, did not want to employ, or could not afford to employ – a Titian or Tintoretto.

On the other hand his sensitiveness gave him an appreciation of shades of feeling that would have escaped Titian's notice. Titian never painted a single figure that does not have the look and bearing, rank and circumstance require. His people are well-bred, dignified, conforming perfectly to current standards. We cannot find fault with Titian for having painted nothing but prosperity, beauty and health – men on parade, as it were – but the interest he himself arouses in the world he painted, makes us eager to know more of these people than he tells us: to know them more intimately, in their own house, if possible,

subject to the wear and tear of ordinary existence. We long to know how they take life, what they think and, above all, what they feel; Titian tells us none of these things, and if we are to satisfy our curiosity, we must turn to Lotto, who is as personal as Titian is typical. If artists were at all conscious of their aims in the 16th century as they are supposed to be now, we might imagine Titian asking of every person he was going to paint: '*Who are you? What is your position in society?*' while *Lotto* would put the question: '*What sort of person are you? How do you take life?*'
BERENSON

No.314: Titian: *John the Baptist*
Room X
No.725: Tintoretto: *Jesus Presented at the Temple*
No.400: Titian: *Pietà*
This is his last work. Intended as an altarpiece for his own tomb in the Frari church, it was left unfinished at his death in 1576 and completed by Palma il Giovane (note the smoother style of the flying angel, the face of the Sibyl on the right, the pediment). The freedom in the handling of the paint owes something to Titian's habit, in later life, of applying paint with his hands.
No.213: Tintoretto: *Crucifixon*
No.245: Tintoretto: *Portrait of Soranzo*

Titian was too busy with commissions for foreign princes to supply the great demand there was (for portraits) in Venice alone. Not only with much of the air of good breeding of Titian's likenesses, but with even greater splendour, and with an astonishing rapidity of execution. The Venetian portrait, it will be remembered was expected to be more than a likeness. It was expected to give pleasure to the eye, and to stimulate emotions. Tintoretto was ready to give ample satisfaction to all such expectations. His portraits, although they are not so individualised as Lotto's, nor such close studies of character as Titian's, always render the man at his best, in glowing health, full of life and determination. They give us the sensuous pleasure we get from jewels, and at the same time they make us look back with amazement to a State where the human plant was in such vigour as to produce old men of the kind represented in most of Tintoretto's portraits.
BERENSON

No.42: Tintoretto: *Saint Mark Rescues Slave from Torture*

The Middle Ages believed that saints worked miracles after their deaths. This painting depicts the legend of the pious servant who despite the prohibitions of his master made a pilgrimage from his native Provence to the Basilica of San Marco in Venice. On his return, the master ordered his eyes to be put out, his legs cut off and his mouth to be beaten with a heavy hammer. The saint intervened and the master subsequently repented. (Cf the more static depictions of these events in Sansovino's bronze reliefs, p.40).

Against the varied cerulean field of the background sky, descending from the olive-green of the foliage at the upper frame, the figure of the saint himself establishes what may be called the basic operational colour notes of the composition: the crimson-mauve of his garment and the gold of his cloak. Distributed throughout the picture – most significantly muted in the costume of the officiating noble enthroned at the right and, at the left frame, shared by the foremost spectator perched upon a column base and the curious mother below – these form a central component of the picture's chromatic structure. Similarly, the olive-green is spread from the central figure holding up the broken hammer, and the azure blue of the sky is distributed below, modified in brilliance and saturation, in various figures from the kneeling torturer to the cap of the mailed onlooker at the left. Run through a full range of variations of hue, modified as they participate in the tonalism of the image's plastic structure, and, finally, set off by the brilliant passages of bravura painting in the reflective armour, such colour relationships constitute a fundamental aspect of the picture's organization. Indeed, in its clarity and intelligence of chromatic construction, the *Miracle of St Mark* is something of a demonstration piece – not so much a tour de force as, literally, a quite finished 'masterpiece,' the public announcement of a young painter's ambitious control of his art.

Commissioned to fill the space between two windows on the short wall of the *sala grande* of the Scuola di San Marco, Tintoretto's canvas received its primary illumination from the windows along the adjacent wall to its left (the observer's right). And, following traditional Renaissance practice, the composition's internal lighting acknowledges this fact of the site, as the forms are illuminated from that side. Within the scene, however, this natural light is eclipsed by the divine radiance of St Mark's halo, which, touching none of the other forms or figures in the picture, finds its correspondence only in the illuminated body of the pious victim below – just as the saint's position in space is reflected in the latter's reverse foreshortening.

ROSAND

An interesting derivative detail of the work is the gateway at the back over which the sculptured figures recline, for these obviously were suggested by casts, which we know Tintoretto to have possessed, of Michael Angelo's tombs in S. Lorenzo's sacristy at Florence. Every individual in the picture is alive and breathing, but none more remarkably so than the woman on the left with a child in her arms and her knee momentarily resting on a slope of the pillar. No doubt some of the crowd are drawn, after the fashion of the time, from public men in Venice; but I know not if they can now be identified.

LUCAS

No.31 : Tintoretto : *Carrying off Body of Saint Mark*
No.203 : Veronese : *Feast in the House of Levy*

Verona, being a dependency of Venice, did no ruling and certainly not at all so
much thinking as Venice, and life there continued healthful, simple,
unconscious, untroubled by the approaching storm of the world's feelings. But
although thought and feeling may be slow in invading a town, fashion comes
there quickly. Spanish fashions in dress, and Spanish ceremonial in manner
reached Verona soon enough, and in Paolo Caliari [Veronese] we find all these
fashions reflected, but health, simplicity, and unconsciousness as well. This
combination of seemingly opposite qualities forms his great charm for us to-day,
and it must have proved as great an attraction to many of the Venetians of his
own time, for they were already far enough removed from simplicity to
appreciate to the full his singularly happy combination of ceremony and
splendour with an almost childlike naturalness of feeling . . . it is curious to note
that Paolo's chief employers were the monasteries. His cheerfulness, and his
frank and joyous worldliness, the qualities, in short, which we find in his huge
pictures of feasts, seem to have been particularly welcome to those who were
expected to make their meat and drink of the very opposite qualities. This is no
small comment on the times, and shows how thorough had been the permeation
of the spirit of the Renaissance, when even the religious orders gave up their
pretence to asceticism and piety.
BERENSON

The measure of the anachronism of Veronese's art is clearly indicated by the
fact that one of his pictures, the vast *'Feast in the House of Simon'*, was the
occasion of his being arraigned before the Inquisition. For it seems in the first
place anachronistic that anyone so urbane and perfectly balanced as Veronese
(to judge by his work) should even be contemporary with such an institution.
Furthermore, it is quite clear from the trial to what extent his picture, which
we may perhaps regard as his masterpiece was out of keeping with the official
ecclesiastical requirements of the time. The minutes of the trial, by remarkable
good fortune, are preserved and constitute fascinating first-hand evidence of the
painter's intentions.
     The gist of the Inquisitors' complaint was that in this picture Veronese had
painted a dog, when the Scriptures said there should be a Magdalen, and that
he had introduced figures of German soldiers, buffoons and dwarfs for which
there was no warrant in the biblical source at all. Veronese begins his defence by
saying that since Simon, the owner of the house, was a rich man it is likely that
he would have had numerous servants. But when questioned specifically about
the buffoon with the parrot (left centre) he says categorically that he merely
put it in for the purposes of decoration, that the canvas was a large one and that
he considered himself at liberty to introduce such additional figures as he
pleased.
     The fact that in the end Veronese was ordered to make changes in the
picture (which he did merely by changing the title to 'Feast in the House of
Levi') is the least significant part of the affair. What is more interesting is the
painter's attitude as revealed in his evidence. It is virtually that of the
Renaissance. It takes beauty as its criterion rather than that spiritual

forcefulness which was *'de rigueur'* in this, the strictest period of the Counter-Reformation (1573). And, indeed, the picture has every quality of High Renaissance art. The composition in its parallel planes, is as rational as that of the School of Athens and the individual figures so easy and graceful in their movements. The lighting is clear, pale and lucid, in contrast to Tintoretto's magical illumination and (sometimes) his bright orange skies. The whole accent is on worldly splendour – on the magnificence of the aristocratic life with fine furnishings and superb velvet and silk clothes and set against a palatial background. The architecture portrayed, indeed, has an interest of its own in view of Veronese's historical position. The main arcade, with its ample half-columns and its sculptured spandrels, is in an idiom which started with Sansovino's library at Venice and was developed by Sanmicheli and by Palladio.

GOULD

No.217: Tintoretto: *Deposition*

In some ways the clearest impression of the essential strangeness of Tintoretto's art, both in its formal characteristics and in its content, may be derived from a comparison of his version of the *'Intombment of Christ'* with that by Titian.[1] Both pictures may be considered masterpieces but they display the most extreme differences of approach.

Titian disposes his figures fairly closely but there is not the slightest uncertainty of the relative positions of any of them. The feet of the three male bearers are clearly seen and we can also see exactly how the Mary's on the left relate to them. But in Tintoretto's picture the figures are densely compressed. . . . We cannot see how there would be space for them all, nor are we meant to do so. Furthermore Tintoretto uses a disquieting device to bring us in close contact with the subject. . . . The drapery under Christ's feet comes almost to the edge of the picture, so that His feet themselves would actually project through the picture plane. The contrast in the content of the two pictures is even more striking. Titian shows us a variety of emotions – the bearer holding Christ's feet displays a stoical grief, St. John behind is almost overcome and turns away. The Virgin advances timidly and pathetically, her trembling mouth slightly open. The Magdalen faces the body with a troubled but firmer expression. With Tintoretto there is not only no contrast of expression, no emotion is shown on the faces at all. His figures are abstractions. Several of the faces are strongly foreshortened or in shadow, and where we can see them clearly they are masks. . . . Even with the hands, which can often be used not only as an adjunct to facial expression but even as a substitute for it, Tintoretto makes but little play. Those of the male Saint are concealed, like his features, those of the Mary who stands at the foot of the Cross make a completely impersonal gesture of despair, while the Madonna's right, though very impressive in its context, is as limp and expressionless as her face. The emotional impact, which is very great, of the picture as a whole derives from this very passivity, from the grouping of the figures in space and from the dramatic and mysterious illumination, and this in general is the rule with Tintoretto.

_____

[1] No.400, beyond entrance door.

The denial implicit in this attitude of the importance of man as an individual together with the utter other-worldliness of the world created by Tintoretto's fantastic light, isolates his art alike from that of the Renaissance and the Baroque. To the Renaissance, man is a noble creature and each representative of the race a unique creation. To the Baroque, man is a hero, bigger, stronger and more vigorous than life and not subject to petty failings. In both cases the world he inhabits is healthy, sunlit and lacking in mysterious or ghostly implications. In both cases, too, human emotions, such as bravery, fear, pride, or humility, even if stereotyped in accordance with the idiom of the Grand Manner, are an essential part of the respective languages. But to Tintoretto, man is of no consequence as an individual. His personal emotions are minimized because they are of the smallest importance. He is merely one of a nameless herd of puppets who carry out the destiny imposed on them by God.
GOULD

Room XI

No.1324: Veronese: *Marriage of Saint Catherine*
No.260: Veronese: *Annunciation*
No.751: Luca Giordano: *Crucifixion of Saint Peter*
No.837: G. B. Tiepolo: *Spandrel with Architecture and Praying Figures*
No.462: G. B. Tiepolo: *Saint Helena Discovering Cross*
No.836: G. B. Tiepolo: *Spandrel*
No.41: Tintoretto: *Cain and Abel*
No.252: Bassano: *Raising of Lazarus*

At an early date the Venetians had perfected an art in which there is scarcely any intellectual content whatever, and in which colour, jewel-like or opaline, is almost everything. Venetian glass was at the same time an outcome of the Venetians' love of sensuous beauty and a continual stimulant to it. Pope Paul II, for example, who was a Venetian, took such a delight in the colour and glow of jewels, that he was always looking at them and always handling them. When painting, accordingly, had reached the point where it was no longer dependent upon the Church, nor even expected to be decorative, but when it was used purely for pleasure, the day could not be far distant when people would expect painting to give them the same enjoyment they received from jewels and glass. In Bassano's works this taste found full satisfaction. Most of his pictures seem at first as dazzling, then as cooling and soothing, as the best kind of stained glass; while the colouring of details, particularly of those under high lights, is jewel-like, as clear and deep and satisfying as rubies and emeralds.

It need scarcely be added after all that has been said about light and atmosphere in connection with Titian and Tintoretto, and their handling of real life, that Bassano's treatment of both was even more masterly. If this were not so, neither picture-fanciers of his own time, nor we nowadays, should care for his works as we do. They represent life in far more humble phases than even the pictures of Tintoretto, and, without recompensing effects of light and atmosphere, they would not be more enjoyable than the cheap work of the smaller Dutch master. It must be added, too, that without his jewel-like colouring, Bassano would often be no more delightful than Teniers.
BERENSON

Room XIII
(on right of corridor)
No.233: Tintoretto: *Portrait of Doge Alvise Mocenigo*
No.245: Tintoretto: *Portrait of a Procuratore*
No.897: Tintoretto: *Portrait of a Procuratore*

Room XVII
(on left of corridor)
No.494: Bellotto: *School of San Marco*
No.463: Canaletto: *Portico*

Here the motifs are not specifically Venetian at all and Canaletto turns back to
the theatrical architectural settings of his youth, though sprinkling the scene
still with touches of genre – like the woman sitting sewing on the right. There is
no obvious effort at fantasy or picturesqueness; the intention is rather to invent
an impressive vista in the grand manner, splendidly lit, and based on the
dignified principles of perspective.
. . . Algarotti had employed Canaletto on those unions of invention and fact
which put the Rialto, the Pantheon and some ruins all together in a caprice
setting. Canaletto's *'morceau de reception'* is something much more ambitious
though not unique in his late work: the creation of a scene which shall appear
realistic but which is in fact totally invented. The result, large, elaborate,
carefully designed and carefully painted, now seems to us (not surprisingly)
academic.
LEVEY

No.709: Guardi: *View of San Giorgio*

Guardi has completely mastered the effects that had been studied by
seventeenth century painters. He has learned that, once we are given the general
impression of a scene, we are quite ready to supply and supplement the details
ourselves. If we look closely at his gondoliers we discover, to our surprise, that
they are made up simply of a few deftly placed coloured patches yet if we step
back the illusion becomes completely effective.
GOMBRICH

No.743: Amigoni: *Venus and Adonis*

The *Venus and Adonis* probably dates from his last stay in Venice, between
1740–47, by which time he was no longer a pioneer of anything, and a fresh
generation of younger men had formulated a more truly rococo style. Against
the new manner, almost exaggerated in its airy elegancies and light-filled
compositions, Amigoni's canvases seem naïve and rather Flemish, and sadly
unpoetical. And though Walpole is often unfair and obtuse in his comments on
foreign painters, when he speaks of Amigoni's manner as a 'still fainter imitation

of that nerveless master Sebastian Ricci' and complains that his figures are
'entirely without expression', it is impossible not to feel that he has put one's
objections very well.
LEVEY

No.741 : Pittoni : *Romans Sacking Temple at Jerusalem*

Pittoni was probably considered rather 'learned' and he presents an
architectural setting more elaborate than most contemporary painters would
have been capable of thinking up. Certainly in eighteenth century France
elaborate classical subjects often had to be planned between the painter and the
Académie des Belles-Lettres. Architectural settings, especially classical ones,
were well worth the trouble of delineating and Madam Geoffrin speaks for her
age when she says of a picture Vien had been commissioned to paint, 'Temples
always make a fine effect by enriching pictures'. The architecture in Pittoni's
painting lends it additional value. The subject also is very noticeably drawn
from history rather than mythology; it is a good deal more serious and elevated
than the love-and-duty themes which were no doubt more popular with
Venetian taste. But it remains a moment of high drama, and offers striking
contrast between the looting Roman soldiery and the distraught aged priests: it
is still an emotional depiction, a clash of will, and the despoiling of an ancient
civilization by a more modern one.
LEVEY

Nos.761–9 : Longhi : *Pictures of Venetian Life*
No.466 : Longhi : *A Concert*

The paint surface is messy, as so often in Longhi; time and practice never
taught him how to apply paint. . . .
　　There is a sort of candour in the slightly ridiculous trio of musical amateurs
and a sort of pungency in the pair of clerical card-players, one thin and eager, the
other fat and porcinely benevolent. . . .
　　Because he is unique it has been presumed that he is invaluable. But it seems
as if his clumsy handling of paint, his inability ever to establish the planes of a
picture, and his incapacity to draw properly, were honest defects that he could
not overcome even after many years of practice.
　　His pictures are therefore, with all their undoubted charm, lazy little pictures:
just as the society he pictures is lazy. The world he sees is in general the enclosed
one of affluent people trying to pass the time. The rooms they inhabit are
enclosed too, and always windowless; they themselves are barely in contact
with each other but are placed, like dolls, in a proximity physical rather than
emotional.
LEVEY

Opposite are some portraits by Rosalba Carriera.

Corridor XIX
(left and left again)
No.107: Basaiti (attr.): *Saint Jerome*
No.645: Basaiti (attr.): *Portrait*
No.90: Carpaccio: *Meeting*
Nos.68 and 68a: Basaiti: *Apostle James* and *Saint Antony Abbot*
No.600: Boccaccio Boccacini: *Marriage of Saint Catherine*

Room XX
No.567: Gentile Bellini: *Procession of the Cross in the Piazza*

The picture, painted in 1500, shows the N arcade – the Procuratie Vecchie – as it had been since 1170. The building we now see was begun in 1514: it has an extra storey, and its detail is entirely c16, but retains the essential character of the earlier building.

The great picture by Gentile Bellini, which shows the progress of the Holy Cross procession across the Piazza in 1496, is historically of much interest. One sees many changes and much that is still familiar. The only mosaic on the façade of St. Mark's which still remains is that in the arch over the left door; and that also is the only arch which has been left concave. The three flagstaffs are there, but they have wooden pediments and no lions on the top, as now. The Merceria clock tower is not yet, and the south arcade comes flush with the campanile's north wall; but I doubt if that was so.[1] The miracle of that year was the healing of a youth who had been fatally injured in the head; his father may be seen kneeling just behind the relic.
LUCAS

No.568: Gentile Bellini: *The Miracle of the Cross*

The Miracle of the Cross . . . depicts the leader of the Brotherhood, Andrea Vendramin, later to become Doge, in the act of miraculously recovering the relics of the Holy Cross that had fallen into the San Lorenzo during a procession.
   Gentile Bellini describes the incident with a charmingly observant story-teller's talent. The figures in the foreground remind us that he is also a shrewd portraitist.
CHASTEL

---

[1] This licence enables us to see the Porta della Carta and part of the Ducal Palace though they are of course in fact hidden from view at this point.

For Gentile Bellini, whose keen eye recorded exactly what he saw, Venice was still a purely Gothic city; witness his famous picture (1500) of the True Cross being retrieved from the Canale di San Lorenzo by Andrea Vendramin (Gallerie dell'Accademia, Venice). This was too prosaic for Carpaccio who, when painting the same episode only a few years earlier,[1] though consenting to show the old wooden Rialto Bridge as it really was, fantastically surmounted by funnel-shaped Gothic chimneys and roof gardens, could not resist the impulse to embellish the foreground by adding a loggia of his own invention – an open gallery typical of the new architecture practiced by Coducci.
PIGNATTI

. . . the Renaissance was a period in the history of modern Europe comparable to youth in the life of the individual. It had all youth's love of finery and of play. The more people were imbued with the new spirit, the more they loved pageants. The pageant was an outlet for many of the dominant passions of the time for there a man could display all the finery he pleased, satisfy his love of antiquity by masquerading as Caesar or Hannibal, his love of knowledge by finding out how the Romans dressed and rode in triumph, his love of glory by the display of wealth and skill in the management of the ceremony, and, above all, his love of feeling himself alive. Solemn writers have not disdained to describe to the minutest details many of the pageants which they witnessed.

Venice, too, knew the love of glory, and the passion was perhaps only the more intense because it was all dedicated to the State. There was nothing the Venetians would not do to add to its greatness, glory, and splendour. It was this which led them to make of the city itself that wondrous monument to the love and awe they felt for their Republic, which still rouses more admiration and gives more pleasure than any other one achievement of the art-impulse in man. They were not content to make their city the most beautiful in the world; they performed ceremonies in its honour partaking of all the solemnity of religious rites. Processions and pageants by land and by sea, free from that gross element of improvisation which characterised them elsewhere in Italy, formed no less a part of the functions of the Venetian State than the High Mass in the Catholic Church. Such a function with Doge and Senators arrayed in gorgeous costumes no less prescribed than the raiments of ecclesiastics, in the midst of the fairy-like architecture of the Piazza or canals, was the event most eagerly looked forward to, and the one that gave most satisfaction to the Venetian's love of his State, and to his love of splendour, beauty, and gaiety. He would have had them every day if it were possible, and to make up for their rarity, he loved to have representations of them. So most Venetian pictures at the beginning of the sixteenth century tended to take the form of magnificent processions, if they did not actually represent them. They are processions in the Piazza, as in Gentile Bellini's 'Corpus Christi' picture or on the water, as in Carpaccio's picture where St. Ursula leaves her home; or they represent what was a gorgeous but common sight in Venice, the reception or dismissal of ambassadors, as in several pictures of Carpaccio's St. Ursula series.[2]

The Mutual Aid Societies – the Schools, as they were called – were not long in getting the masters who were employed in the Doge's Palace to execute for their own meeting places pictures equally splendid.

---

[1] No.566.   [2] Accademia, Room XXI (p.91).

Many of these pictures – most in fact – took the form of pageants; but even in such, intended as they were for almost domestic purposes, the style of high ceremonial was relaxed, and elements taken directly from life were introduced. In his 'Corpus Christi'[1] Gentile Bellini paints not only the solemn and dazzling procession in the Piazza, but the elegant young men who strut about in all their finery, the foreign loungers and even the unfailing beggar by St. Mark's. In 'The Miracle of the True Cross' he introduces gondoliers taking care to bring out all the beauty of their lithe, comely figures as they stand to ply the oar, and does not reject even such an episode as a serving-maid standing in a doorway watching a negro who is about to plunge into the canal. He treats this bit of the picture with all the charm and much of that delicate feeling for simple effects of light and colour that we find in such Dutch painters as Vermeer van Delft and Peter de Hoogh.

BERENSON

The genius of Giovanni Bellini seems to us now so outstanding, and his influence in the Veneto during the opening years of the 16th century so pre-eminent, that it is at first difficult to realise that during the greater part of his life his fame had been eclipsed by that of his brother, Gentile. The latter would have appeared unquestionably the most eminent Venetian painter working in the second half of the century. He was knighted by the Emperor in 1469, summoned by the Sultan to Constantinople ten years later and entrusted with the most important commission in the power of the Venetian State to give – the decoration of the great hall in the Doge's palace. These paintings were destroyed by fire in the 16th century, but sufficient of Gentile's work in general survives to permit us to estimate his talents.

The role played by religion in the Venetian state at the time of the Renaissance was of a uniquely possessive character. . . . This tendency to identify his State with the Christian religion represented one side of the Venetian's character. Another, its love of luxury and general sensuality, is shown in the opulent splendour of the city itself, with its accent on rich materials – many coloured marbles and gold mosaics externally, and gilded wood, damasks and fantastic metal-work and glass in its interiors – and above all, in the pageants which then, as now, served as an occasion for the whole city to flock to the route. As these were usually religious in character they thus combined the two most characteristic elements in Venetian life and we may therefore not be surprised at the popularity of portrayals of them in art. Those of Gentile Bellini were the prototypes, and though we can see from them that he had no fraction of his brother's greatness, his minutely careful rendering of the splendour of Venetian ceremonial was precisely what the circumstances of the moment demanded.

GOULD

No.566: Carpaccio: *The Miracle of the Cross at the Rialto*

The painting is a valuable reconstruction of the Grand Canal as it was at the end of the 15th century.

---

[1] No.567.

The miracle (the healing of a possessed soul) takes place in a loggia decorated with the Roman medallions that were then the last word in 'Classical style' as conceived by the Lombard sculptors; the Vendramin-Calergi Palace which still has its portal decorated with profiles of Roman emperors, is a fine example of this fashion.[1] This type of decorative motif recurs frequently in Carpaccio's works.

The *Miracle at the Rialto* shows the old drawbridge still in existence at the time, the curious silhouettes of the chimneys and the squat gondolas whose shape was to be modified in the 17th century.

CHASTEL

The figure of the black gondolier reminds us that household slaves were a feature of c15 Venice. The economy was never dependent on slaves. Galleys, for example, were manned by paid rowers (after **1540** by prisoners). But the Venetian affection for 'liberty' did not extend to any moral objections to slavery.

These three pictures [in this room] are valuable for the light they throw on the way in which Venetians dressed during the Renaissance and their behavior in official ceremonies. They show us the 'fair-haired men with slim figures, grave, silent tread and careful speech' described by Burckhardt. In this they differed from the other peoples of Italy; to some extent Nordic in their ways, they were nevertheless apt to dress with all the ostentation of orientals when they were not wearing their uniforms of office – which remained unchanged from the Middle Ages to the 18th century.

The normal dress of the solemn, middle-aged patricians of Venice bore no resemblance to the garnish and luxurious costume which so delighted the young men of the time. Basically they dressed in a long gown of black cloth, revealing the collar of a white shirt above the neck clasp. This heavy garment with its wide folds was also worn by the men of the professional classes, and as it reached right to the ground, those who wore it were obliged to walk with a slow, solemn, dignified step. This was the characteristic walk of the bourgeoisie and the aristocracy at a time when only children and workmen were so indiscreet as to run in the streets. On ceremonial occasions, Senators wore gowns of crimson satin, for this was the distinguishing mark of their office.

BRION

Room XXI
(left along corridor)
Carpaccio: *Dream of Saint Ursula*
The cycle was commissioned (in **1490**) for the Scuola di Sant'Ursula: the highly individual faces of the robed figures are believed to be portraits of members of the Scuola. The young men in the paintings represent young

---

[1] See p. 185.   [2] They are decorated with carvings and painted surface-features, says Sally Spector, more Carpaccio's creation than a strict record of reality.

aristocrats, who would be required at 25 to enter the Great Council and wear sober robes, but up to that age belonged to clubs known as Companies of the Hose and disported themselves in gaily-coloured doublet and hose.

All the architecture of the series is delightful, as well as being realistically conceived in terms of space and structure. Most of the buildings are of course invented, but some are based on real ones – No.573 on the interior of the Ducal Palace. In No.575, the palace on the right plainly owes something to the Ca' d'Oro (p.173), and the towers are based on those of Rhodes and Candia, known from late c15 German engravings. No.572: Arrival of the English Ambassadors to propose the marriage between the King's son and Princess Ursula. In her bedroom, Ursula tells her father she intends to go on a pilgrimage.

No.573: The King of Bretagna gives his reply to the Ambassadors.

No.574: The Ambassadors take the reply to England. As Hare remarks, the Venetian idea of England is interesting.

No.575: The Departure.

> Here are three representations. On the right is Ursula with her father, on the left Conon with his. In the centre the pair meet near the ship of their pilgrimage. The background is supposed to give the characteristics of a civilised and a barbaric city.
>
> HARE

No.577: The Engaged Couple arrive in Rome – the Castle of S. Angel in the background.

No.578: The Dream of Saint Ursula. As a girl, she had dreamed that she would devote herself to the service of God.

No.579: The arrival at Cologne, which is being besieged by the Huns.

No.580: The Martyrdom of the Christians, and the Funeral of Ursula.

No.576: Apotheosis of Ursula.

> Certain of the episodes from the cycle painted for the Scuola di Sant'Orsola contain charming descriptions of Venetian interiors of Carpaccio's time.
>
> In the scene showing Ursula and her father[1] there is a canopied bed with embroidered drapery near the picture of the Virgin and Child in a precious frame. And the room where Saint Ursula lies sleeping[2] with the flowers on the sill beneath the small, lead-set window-panes, an open book on the table and a candle stick hung in front of some devotional painting, is the room of a well-bred

---

[1] No.572, right.   [2] No.578.

girl who says her prayers and sets her slippers near her bed before going to sleep. Beyond the doorway, another lighted aperture creates a skilful light effect in the Flemish manner.

The story of St. Ursula is theoretically an illustration of the fabulous career of the saint, but it has always been recognised as providing as accurate a picture of contemporary Venetian life as the avowed representations of ceremonials. One sees how much Carpaccio learnt from Gentile, yet the pedestrian quality of the latter's arrangement of figures in rows is transformed by Giovanni's light which brings to life the different texturesof rich brocades, carpets and pearls, of water shimmering in the sun or cool and transparent in the shadows.

At the same time the increase in pictorial quality is accompanied by a decrease in solemnity. Gentile's figures have always a due sense of the occasion, are always to some extent absorbed in the religious ceremony, no matter how far away from it they may be. But Carpaccio's ladies and gentlemen lounge amorously in gondolas, or indulge in trivial conversation or gossip during a solemn moment. If documentation has become suffused with an element of poetry it would also be true to say that history has become genre.

GOULD

Much as he loved pageants, he loved homelier scenes as well. His 'Dream of St. Ursula'[1] shows us a young girl asleep in a room filled with the quiet morning light. Indeed, it may be better described as the picture of a room with the light playing softly upon its walls, upon the flower-pots in the window, and upon the writing-table and the cupboards. A young girl happens to be asleep in the bed, but the picture is far from being a merely economic illustration of this episode in the life of the saint. Again, let us take the work in the same series[2] where King Maure dismisses the ambassadors. Carpaccio has made this a scene of a chancellery in which the most striking features are neither the king, nor the ambassadors, but the effect of the light that streams through a side door on the left and a poor clerk labouring at his task.

Carpaccio's quality is the quality of the painter of 'genre' of which he was the earliest Italian master. His 'genre' differs from Dutch or French not in kind but in degree. Dutch 'genre' is much more democratic, and, as painting, is of a far finer quality, but it deals with its subject, as Carpaccio does, for the sake of its own pictorial capacities and for the sake of the effects of colour and of light and shade.

BERENSON

Room XXII
(return along corridor)
No.592: Cima da Conegliano: *Tobias and Angel*
No.604: Cima da Conegliano: *Deposition*
No.603: Cima da Congliano: *Madonna and Child*

---

[1] No.578.   [2] No.573.

Behind first screen
Nos.83, 84, 86: Benedetto Diana: *Madonna and Saints*

On second screen
No.82: Benedetto Diana: *Madonna and Saints*

On right wall beside second screen
No.823: Lazzaro Bastiani: *Funeral of Saint Jerome*

Behind second screen
No.618: Alvise Vivarini: *John the Baptist*
No.607: Alvise Vivarini: *Sacred Conversation*

Alvise was a rather crude, but forceful painter. There is no finesse in his draughtsmanship, and his colours are muddy. But he seems to have had a passion for the 3-dimensional element, and used the discoveries in lighting to this end. His Child is so plastic that combined with the unrefined draughtsmanship, He looks like a rubber figure blown up to bursting point. By shutting out the background, furthermore (by means of the curtain) and crowding the strongly-lit figures closely together round the Madonna's throne (itself very narrow) as though, having insufficient space within the picture, they would burst out on to the spectator, one is uncomfortably aware of the 3-dimensional element as if one were looking through stereoscopic spectacles.
GOULD

Nos.593, 593a, 619: Alvise Vivarini: *Saints*

On right wall beside second screen
No.103: Crivelli: *Saints Jerome and Augustine*
No.103a: Crivelli: *Saints Peter and Paul*

Central apse
Nos.621, 621a, 621b, 621c: Giovanni Bellini: *Four Triptychs*

Left chapel
No.105: Crivelli: *Four Saints*
No.100: Bastiani: *Il Presepe*
No.734: Giovanni Bellini: *Annunciation*

Last room
No.626: Titian: *Presentation of the Virgin*
This large canvas was painted for its present site – then the *albergo* (a kind

of committee room) of a *scuola*. The doorway on the right was already there (see the masonry depicted over it); the left doorway was made later in the c16.

The Presentation of the Virgin . . . started about 1534 . . . which reverts to an older scheme of iconograpny such as had already been used, among others, by Cima, is (apart from certain works by Veronese) the last major painting entirely in the High Renaissance classical tradition executed anywhere in Italy. It represents, indeed, a strange reversion by Titian after his proto-Baroque phase initiated by the *Assunta*.[1] The figures, all arranged parallel with the picture plane, are spaced in a completely rational and lucid manner, and the colouring and lighting are serenity and calm.
GOULD

It is still in the place for which it was executed between 1534 and 1538. This place is one of the long walls of the Albergo, or committee-room, of the Scuola della Carità. This is an innovation: one large picture, instead of a series of histories, filling the space between stalls and ceiling. On the left a large rectangle was cut out when a second door was made in the seventeenth century; this has considerably affected the balance of the composition. Otherwise the condition of the painting is very good. In this long, tapestry-like picture groups have been arranged in shallow strata which are defined by the architecture. The groups follow one after another in a somewhat loose order, and they differ from the close-knit units of the works of about 1520. One has to read the composition figure by figure from left to right; the eye may rest for a while on some beautiful detail and then move on slowly, in the same tempo in which the little Mary is ascending the stairs with dignity and nobility. 'Piccola Maria' – this is the nick-name of this very popular picture in Venice – is dressed in light-blue, and is surrounded by a golden halo. Now, these two colours are those of the original coffered ceiling of the Albergo. They also recur in many other places in the picture, set among other jewel-like deep colours. The antique torso and the market woman, to right and left of the original door, seem to belong to a different reality; they are a natural link between the spectator and the gay and solemn world depicted.
WILDE

Peggy Guggenheim Collection

Outside the Accademia, turn right and right again; then left into Calle Nova Sant'Agnese. The way continues back to the entrance of the Peggy Guggenheim Collection (open 12.00–18.00; closed Tuesday; free Saturday 18.00–21.00). The museum is the former house of Peggy Guggenheim

---

[1] In the Frari church, p.144.

and contains her collection of c20 painting and sculpture, outstandingly well presented and catalogued.

We may return to the Piazza by traghetto to Santa Maria del Giglio or by vaporetto from the Salute.

Il fait bon voir (Magny) ces Coïons magnifiques,
Leur superbe Arcenal, leurs vaisseaux, leur abbord,
Leur Sainct Marc, leur Palais, leur Realte, leur port,
Leurs changes, leurs profits, leurs banques et leurs trafiques.

Il fait bon voir le bec de leurs chapprons antiques,
Leurs robbes à grand'manche et leurs bonnets sans bord,
Leur parler tout grossier, leur gravité, leur port,
Et leurs sages avis aux affaires publiques.

Il fait bon voir de tout leur Senat balloter,
Il fait bon voir par tout leurs gondolles flotter,
Leurs femmes, leurs festins, leur vivre solitaire :

Mais ce que l'on en doit meilleur estimer,
C'est quand ces vieux coquz vont espouser la mer,
Dont ils sont les maris et le Ture l'adultère.
DU BELLAY

Walk 3

San Zaccaria – Arsenal – S. Giorgio degli Schiavoni

This walk is in two parts. San Zaccaria does not open for visitors until 10 a.m.; the first half makes a leisurely walk with a late start. Readers who are content to omit some of the detail may do this walk in one morning; others should terminate at the Arsenal and begin again at that point.

From the Piazza, take the Porta della Carta (to the right of the Basilica of San Marco) into the courtyard of the Doge's Palace. Note the round arches on the lower level and the pointed ones above (referred to by Lieberman – p.100). Leave the courtyard through the gateway in the middle of the far side and turn left along the Riva degli Schiavoni – in front of the Ducal Palace. The last two lines in the poem opposite – addressed by Joachim du Bellay to his friend Olivier de Magny – are

> . . . a humerous reference to the famous 'Sposalizio del Mar' – Wedding of the Sea, an annual ceremony of great pomp in which the Doge cast a ring into the Adriatic and paid homage to the seas as the instrument of Venetian wealth and grandeur – and a sly allusion to the rising naval power of the Ottoman Turks, who by then, whether adulterously or not, had virtually supplanted Venice in the fickle graces of the Mediterranean.
> PIGNATTI

Before you cross the Ponte della Paglia you can see on the side of the bridge a little tabernacle with c16 relief – the Madonna of the Gondoliers. Just before the next bridge, on the left – a c15 palazzo now the Danieli Hotel.

> It is true that Alfred de Musset, when he paid a catastrophic visit to Venice with George Sand, who promptly ran off with a handsome young doctor – it is quite true that de Musset occupied Room 13 at the Hotel Danieli ('Alfred was a sad flirt,' said Swinburne, 'and George was no gentleman').
> MORRIS

The building is perhaps more distinguished as the site of the performance of the first opera in Venice – Monteverdi's *Proserpina Rapita*.

San Zaccaria

Go over the bridge, and then left under the archway after Hotel Savoia e
Jolanda into a small campo, dominated by the c15 façade of the church of
San Zaccaria (open 10.00–12.00; 16.00–18.00 – organ and other features
restored by the Dutch Committee).

It is a very tall church, much too tall for its width by the canons of classical
architecture, and its Gothic skeleton is barely disguised by an incrustation of
Renaissance motifs. Begun by Antonio Gambello in the 1440s, it was completed
in the last two decades of the century by Mauro Coducci who designed three tiers
of round-headed windows and shell-capped niches crowned by a curious
semicircular pediment. It is easy to see how this façade must have appealed to
the Venetians, for while it was up to date in classical detail it yet retained the
opulent elaboration of the flamboyant Gothic style. But whereas the façade is the
result of a successful compromise, the interior suggests a state of hostility. The
proportions of this lofty church and its plan – with a screen round the high altar,
an ambulatory and apsidal chapels – are Gothic. But most of the decorations are
outspokenly Renaissance. Behind the elegant Gothic screen surrounding the high
altar there is open warfare, where octagonal Gothic piers suddenly develop into
Corinthian half-columns.
HONOUR

When Codussi took over at San Zaccaria in 1483 the façade had progressed only as
far as the lower story. In the upper levels Codussi rejected the rich colourism of
Gambello's ground storey in favour of Istrian stone. Only in the uppermost levels,
in the friezes of the top entablature and the pediment, did he use coloured marble
and polychrome inserts in any quantity.
   Where the decorative corner elements of the projecting buttresses of Gambello's
ground storey were very slender twisted colonnettes stacked up three to a storey,
Codussi's decoration is much larger in scale; on the third level of the façade there
are two tall free-standing columns at the corners of each buttress. The row of shell
niches on the second storey of the façade is Codussi's inspired transition from
Gambello's ground storey to his own upper levels of the façade.
LIEBERMAN

Inside the church, the columns, capitals and ceiling deserve special
notice.

---

*The Riva degli Schiavoni engraved in 1754 by Vissentini from Canaletto's
drawing may be compared with the view Canaletto did some ten years earlier
(p.25): In the middle-ground can be seen a C15 palazzo, now the Danieli
Hotel. The extension of the fondamenta beyond the Ponte della Paglia had
been completed when the drawing below was done in 1843. The buildings to
the left of the Danieli have been replaced by an extension of the hotel.*

The nave is a very characteristic example of how the Byzantine manner of
spreading cycles of paintings like carpets over the walls continued in Venice even
in post-Byzantine art.
DECKER

On right, entrance to chapel of St Athanasius (admission charge).

On altar
Tintoretto: *Birth of Saint John*

Over entrance
Van Dyck (attr.): *Crucifixion*

From this chapel go through to chapel of St Tarasius

Altar piece (from left to right)
G. and A. da Murano: *Saint Mark*
Plebanus di S. Agnese: *Saint Blaise*
Plebanus di S. Agnese: *Virgin.*
Plebanus di S. Agnese: *Saint Martin*
G. and A. da Murano: *Saint Elisabeth*

On wall on left of altar
G. and A. da Murano: *Altarpiece*

The floor in front of the main altar remains from the c12 church; above
the apse are Andrea del Castagno's frescoes representing God the Father,
Four Evangelists, St Zacharias and John the Baptist. The figures stand
out firmly, in the high relief manner characteristic of mid-c15 Florence.
Beneath the glass at the other end of the chapel, you can see the remains
of an older floor c9. The stairs lead to the crypt. The floor may be under
water.
    Back into main church, follow the ambulatory round behind the high
altar.

There are striking differences in style and scale between the semicircular chapels
and the two-storey arcade around the choir. The decoration of the chapels, with
niches formed by wall columns carrying undecorated arches, is derived from San
Marco...
    The choir is a combination of Gothic and Classical forms that, although a bit
more extreme, is similar to several examples from the period. Despite the unusual
mixed vocabulary, some features can be related to Venetian traditions: the single
arches of the lower level and the divided arches above preserve the rhythm of the
Procuratie Vecchie; the combination of round arches on the lower level and

pointed arches above was used in the east courtyard façade of the Palazzo Ducale
in the 1480s
LIEBERMAN

Coming down the N aisle of the church, we find on the wall Giovanni
Bellini: *Virgin Enthroned*

The painters of the Middle Ages were no more concerned about the 'real' colours
of things than they were about their real shapes. In the miniatures, enamel work
and panel paintings, they loved to spread out the purest and most precious
colours they could get with shining gold and flawless ultramarine blue as a
favourite combination. The great reformers of Florence were less interested in
colour than in drawing. That does not mean, of course, that their pictures were
not exquisite in colour – the contrary is true – but few of them regarded colour
as one of the principal means of welding the various figures and forms of a
picture into one unified pattern. They preferred to do this by means of
perspective and composition before they even dipped their brushes into paint.
The Venetian painters, it seems, did not think of colour as an additional
adornment for the picture after it had been drawn on the panel. When one enters
the little church of San Zaccaria in Venice and stands before the picture which
the great Venetian painter Giovanni Bellini had painted over the altar there in
1505 in his old age, one immediately notices that his approach to colour was very
different. Not that the picture is particularly bright or shining. It is rather the
mellowness and richness of the colours that impress one before one even begins
to look at what the picture represents. I think that even a photograph conveys
something of the warm and gilded atmosphere which fills the niche in which the
Virgin sits enthroned, with the infant Jesus lifting His little hand to bless the
worshippers before the altar. An angel at the foot of the altar softly plays the
violin while the saints stand quietly at either side of the throne: St. Peter with
his key and book, St. Catherine with the palm of martyrdom and the broken
wheel. St. Apollonia and St. Jerome, the scholar who translated the Bible into
Latin, and whom Bellini therefore represented as reading in a book. Many
Madonnas with saints have been painted before and after, in Italy and elsewhere,
but few were ever conceived with such dignity and repose. In the earlier days,
the picture of the Virgin used to be rigidly flanked by the traditional images of
the saints. Bellini knew how to bring life into a simple symmetrical arrangement
without upsetting its order. He also knew how to turn the traditional figures of
the Virgin and saints into real and living beings without divesting them of their
old character and dignity. He did not even sacrifice the variety and
individuality of real life, as Perugino had done to some extent. St. Catherine
with her dreamy smile, and St. Jerome, the old scholar engrossed in his book,
are real enough in their own ways, although they, too, no less than Perugino's
figures, seem to belong to another more serene and beautiful world, a world
transfused with that warm and supernatural light that fills the picture.
GOMBRICH

To the Virgin's right stand St. Catherine and St. Peter, to her left St. Lucy and
St. Jerome, while through the arches on each side we look out on to a narrow
strip of landscape, showing plants, trees, distant mountains, and cloud-flecked

sky. All is informed and unified by a soft envelope of light, which fuses the colours red and pink, blue and grey, orange, brown, green, and gold into a single whole, yet letting them retain their individual identity and purity. . . .
ROBERTSON

It contains seven nearly life-size figures; five are seen squarely from the front, two – and these are links between the sections of the tripartite composition – are seen in profile; that is to say, even more clearly than in the *Baptism* all the figures have been arranged parallel to the picture plane. They are considerably broadened by their draperies, that is to say by forms which are merely optical or visual supports, and which make for a unified surface; notice how the garments of the two main saints merge into those of their neighbours. The architecture though still of the same system as in earlier compositions of this type (that is to say, continuing the real architecture of the altar-frame), is seen in a perspective which makes the half-cylinder of the apse appear as a shallow niche owing to the great distance from which it is viewed. The viewpoint has also been raised well above the spectator's level, and thus the representation has lost its illusionistic effect: it has become something objective. Symmetry and a regular alternation of bright and dark colours prevail in the whole. All these qualities make this reunion of saints timeless. There are few pictures in Venice in which the classical ideal of a pure and calm existence is as fully realized as here.
WILDE

Back to the Riva degli Schiavoni: turn left and go over the next bridge – Ponte della Pietà (leaning campanile of San Giorgio dei Greci visible on left) – to the c18 church of the Pietà, oval in plan with vaulted ceiling and ambulatory (structure, organ and ceiling paintings restored, IFM).

Inside, ceiling fresco
G. B. Tiepolo: *The Triumph of Faith (Coronation of Virgin)*

Continue along the Riva degli Schiavoni, over the next bridge, and left into the narrow Calle del Dose. This emerges in front of the late c15 church of San Giovanni in Bragora.

On the wall of the N aisle, beyond the second chapel
Alvise Vivarini: *Madonna and Child*

On the high altar
Cima da Conegliano: *Baptism of Jesus*

At the E end of the S aisle, we find on the wall
Alvise Vivarini: *Resurrection of Jesus*
Cima da Conegliano: *Constantine Holding the Cross*

Right outside the church and out of the campo immediately on the right –
down Calle Va in Crosera; left at Calle del Pestrin, over the iron bridge
into the Campo San Martino. On the right is the c16 church of San
Martino, by Sansovino (restored, Australian Committee). It has an
impressive organ and c17 and c18 illusionistic ceiling. In the choir behind
the main altar
Palma il Giovane: *Flagellation* (N)
Palma il Giovane: *Way to Calvary* (S)

Arsenal

Continue along the fondamenta to the Arsenal. This shipyard was
formerly of great importance, and the basis of the Republic's sea power
and trade. Founded in 1104, by the c16 it had become the largest
industrial plant of its time, occupying over 60 acres and employing more
than 16,000 people, and pioneering the use of standardised parts and
assembly-line production. Piranesi (1720–78), though he lived most of his
adult life in Rome, visited the Arsenal as a young man; Sally Spector
suggests that the thick ropes, suspended bridges, iron rings and pulleys
hung in vast, vaulted spaces influenced his etching series *The Prisons*.
The shipyard continued to be used until the First World War, towards
the end of which it was demolished for fear it would fall into enemy hands.
It has remained unused since. It is the one major Venetian monument
mentioned in the *Divine Comedy*; fittingly, its gateway has been restored
by the Dante Alighieri Society of Rome. The impressive towers have been
repointed; the *Madonna and Child* (attributed to Sansovino) in the
vestibule has been restored; generally, this is an important piece of
restoration.

Outside the main gates of the Arsenal, among a pride of peers, there stands a tall
marble lion,[1] gangling but severe. This beast was brought from Athens in 1687
by the fighting Doge Francesco Morosini (chiefly eminent in universal history
because a shell from one of his ships exploded the Turkish powder magazine that
happened to be inside the Parthenon). The lion used to guard the gateway into
the Piraeus, and was so celebrated among the ancients that the port itself was
known as the Port of the Lion: but when it arrived at the Arsenal, booty of war,
the Venetians were puzzled to discover that engraved upon its shoulders and
haunches were some peculiar inscriptions, not at all Greek in style, in characters
that seemed to the eyes of a people accustomed to the exquisite calligraphies of
Arabic, rudely and brusquely chiselled. For several centuries nobody knew what
these letters were: until one nineteenth century day a visiting Danish scholar

---

[1] On the left of gateway.

inspected them, raised his arms in exultation, and pronounced them to be Norse runes. They were carved on the lion in the eleventh century by order of Harold the Tall, a Norwegian mercenary who fought several campaigns in the Mediterranean, conquering Athens and once dethroning the Emperor in Constantinople, only to die in 1066 as King of Norway, fighting Harold the Saxon at Stamford Bridge, Yorkshire. The inscription on the lion's left shoulder says: 'Haakon, combined with Ulf, with Asmud and with Orn, conquered this port. These men and Harold the Tall imposed large fines, on account of the revolt of the Greek people. Dalk has been detained in distant lands. Egil was waging war, together with Ragnar, in Roumania and Armenia.' And on the right haunch of this queer animal is inscribed, in the runic: 'Asmund engraved these runes in combination with Asgeir, Thorleif, Thord and Ivar, by desire of Harold the Tall, although the Greeks on reflection opposed it.'
MORRIS

The Arsenale portal carries the date 1460 on the pedestals.[1] The inscription on the frieze and some commemorative sculpture were added in the 16th century. Originally there was a small drawbridge leading to the gate; the fixed bridge and small enclosure in front of it are 17th-century additions.

The Venetians' view of themselves as 'new Romans' received its clearest architectural expression at the Arsenale. As the heart of the city's naval life, both military and mercantile, the Arsenale was a place of fundamental importance for Venetians, and to emphasize the idea of Roman inheritance the entrance to the maritime centre was through a Roman gate. It is interesting that the capitals of the ground-level columns are not Classical, but 12th-century Byzantine pieces in re-use. The architecture thus fuses the two sources of Venetian culture into a single work.

At the Arsenale the paired columns on pedestals, and the entablature that breaks forward over them, are derived from the Arch of the Sergii in Pula ... but while at Pula the piers of the central arch rise from pedestals as high as those supporting the columns, at the Arsenale they rise directly from ground level, as they do in triumphal arches in Rome and Verona.

For the upper part of the Arsenale portal the architect had no Roman model to draw on, and this level is not Classical. Its contrast with the lower storey is interesting, and the overall design may be subtler than it first appears. The idea may have been to imitate those cases in which Roman architecture was re-used. Perhaps we are meant to suspend disbelief so far as to imagine that the Arsenale was built around a Roman arch to which a top storey was added in a different, later style. Venetian historical myths would have been well served by such a notion.
LIEBERMAN

On the right of the gateway, the middle lion brought here from Delos in c18 is Greek, c6 B.C. (head added later).

---

[1] right pedestal.

S. Giorgio dei Greci.

Those terminating the walk here may take the vaporetto from the Riva degli Schiavoni (over the wooden bridge in front of the Arsenal towers, turn right, and right again over the bridge). Return the same way for the second half of the walk.

S. Giorgio degli Schiavoni

From the Arsenal take the calle which runs to the left of the gateway (Calle del Pestrin), turn right at No.3892 – Calle dei Corazzeri; left through the campo, right into Salizzada San Antonin; just before bridge, right along Fondamenta dei Furlani to c16 San Giorgio degli Schiavoni. Ground floor – series of paintings by Carpaccio. (Restored 1970 by the Comitato Italiano per Venezia. Charge for admission. Open 9.30–12.30 every day; 15.30–18.30 weekdays; closed Monday).

This is a *scuola* – the first of seven we visit in these walks. The scuole were guilds whose members were of the social class below that of the aristocracy.

Starting from the left
Carpacccio: *Scenes from the Life of Saint George*
1. *Saint George killing the dragon*
2. *Triumph of Saint George*
3. *Saint George Baptising Eastern King*
The red parrot, Philip Rylands believes, is the first evidence in western art of the discovery of the Americas. The Virgin and Child on the altar is also attributed to Carpaccio.

After the altar, continuing to the right
Carpaccio: *Saint Tryphone Subdues a Demon in the Form of a Basilisk*

On the right wall
Carpaccio:
1. *Agony in the Garden*
2. *The Calling of Saint Matthew*
3. *Saint Jerome Leads the Tamed Lion to the Monastery*
4. *Funeral of Saint Jerome*
5. *Saint Augustine of Hippo*
He is receiving the revelation of Saint Jerome's death while in the act of writing to him. The figure was formerly believed to be Saint Jerome.

The church of San Francesco della Vigna, drawn by Luca Carlevaris (1663–1731) about 1725, shows the characteristic Palladio façade on the west front which was superimposed on Jacopo Sansovino's (1486–1570) original design.

Carpaccio's Saint Jerome in his Cell depicts a Venetian scholar's pleasant studio rather than the austere retreat of an ascetic. The Saint, clothed in a scarlet cape and white surplice, sits writing at an elegant desk. Manuscripts in costly red bindings and musical scores lie scattered about. The sea-shell on the table attests to the fondness for curios, strange objects and bizarre natural formations which was typical of the period. Capaccio does not omit the armillary sphere – for interest in astronomy was widespread among cultivated people – nor above all, the collector's shelves (on the left-hand wall). Here we make out the small terra cotta vases and bronze statuettes dear to the antique lovers of the time.
CHASTEL

At this point there is an optional excursion to the church of San Francesco della Vigna. It is distinguished by having a façade designed by Palladio and an interior designed by Sansovino, modelled on Cronaca's church of San Salvatore al Monte in Florence (though his design was modified during construction). To reach San Francesco, turn left outside

San Giorgio, along the Calle dei Furlani, left at the end into Campo de le
Gatte: across the campo, left along the Salizzada de le Gatte, Salizzada
San Francesco and Ramo al Ponte San Francesco.

To see the interior as Sansovino intended it, we must bear in mind that
the Istrian stone, now darkened to a sombre grey, was originally white.

The church contains, on the entrance wall, beside entrance door
Antonio Vivarini (attr.): *Three Saints*

Fifth chapel on the right
Chapel of the Barbaro Family

> The Cappella Barbaro was founded by Francesco Barbaro, 1480–1568, to
> contain the ashes of his illustrious ancestors, amidst whom he is buried himself.
> His tomb bears the device – a red circle ('tondo') on a field argent – which was
> granted in 1125 to the Admiral Marco Barbaro, in remembrance of his having,
> during the battle of Ascalon, cut off the hand of a Moor who had seized the flag
> of his vessel, slain him, and turned his turban into a banner, after having traced
> a red circle with his bleeding arm.
> HARE

Chapel in s transept
Standing on c16 altar, altar-piece
Antonio da Negroponte: *Virgin and Child, Enthroned*
(Depiction of *Holy Father*, above, c16 addition)
(restored, Save Venice Inc)

A door in the N transept leads into a corridor. To the left, a delightful
c15 cloister. The chapel opposite contains a panel
Giovanni Bellini (with assistant; the face of the donor is a later c16
substitution): *Virgin and Child, Saints and Donor*

Come back to San Giorgio the same way. Cross the bridge beside the
scuola; turn right along the Fondamenta San Giorgio dei Schiavoni. The
second calle on the left (Calle San Lorenzo) leads into the Campo San
Lorenzo. Cross the bridge at the far end of the campo. This bridge and the
waterways to the right of it were the setting for Bellini's *Miracle of the
Cross*, now in the Accademia (p.87). Turn left along the Fondamenta
Lorenzo, left again over the second bridge (Ponte dei Greci) and
immediately right to the Greek Institute (Istituto Ellenico. Open,
weekdays 9.30–12.30; 15.30–18.00; Sunday 9.00–12.00; closed Tuesday).
The custodian will admit you (admission charge) to a remarkable
collection of Greek icons belonging to the Greek community in Venice.
They are housed in the c17 Scuola di San Nicolò designed by Longhena.

The church of San Giorgio dei Greci and its campanile in 1720. The present condition of the tower can be seen in Kaffe Fasset's drawing on page 105.

Ask to see the oval staircase on the left of the entrance and the assembly hall on the first floor.

In the same courtyard is c16 church of San Giorgio dei Greci, with a c16 leaning campanile (which we saw from the Ponte della Pietà) and small Renaissance loggia; beyond, a c15 well-head; beyond, a small c17 palace, the treasury of the church.

We now return towards the Piazza – over the Ponte dei Greci, along the Fondamenta dell'Osmarin (the view behind is seen in the c18 illustration above) into Campo San Provolo. At the end of the campo, on left, Gothic arch with c15 marble relief. We do not go under this arch (it leads into the Campo San Zaccaria), but go over the Ponte San Provolo to Campo Santi Filipo e Giacomo. Turn right immediately into Calle impeto la Sacrestia (which becomes Calle drio la Chiesa) and then left into Calle a fianco la Chiesa. The c18 church of San Giovanni Novo (generally shut, but verger may sometimes be found) has an interior which is a miniature version of part of the interior of San Giorgio Maggiore (p.17).

We return the way we came, to Campo Santi Filipo e Giacomo and turn right to Ponte di Canonica. The Prison, Bridge of Sighs and Ducal Palace appear on the left. Before going over the bridge, turn left along the canal, and enter No.4312, to see the Romanesque cloister of Sant'Apollonia.

A very interesting small museum upstairs shows recently restored works, among which
Moretto da Brescia: *Jesus at Simon's House*

> ... painted in 1544 for San Fermo, at Monselice, and brought to Venice in 1740. Richard Wagner was so pleased with this work that while in Venice he paid frequent visits to it. In the background is seen the artist's native city.
> HARE

Go along the Fondamenta di Canonica to the point where the private bridge leads to the c16 Palazzo Trevisan (now showrooms for Venetian ceramics).

> In the inlaid design of the dove with the olive-branch of the Casa Trevisan, it is impossible for anything to go beyond the precision with which the olive leaves are cut out of the white marble; and, in some wreaths of laurels below, the rippled edge of each leaf is finely and easily drawn, as if by a delicate pencil. No Florentine table is more exquisitely finished than the façade of this entire palace; and as an ideal of executive perfection, this palace is most notable amidst the architecture of Europe.
> RUSKIN

The Ramo (Calle) di Canonica leads back to the Piazza.

Everyday market-place scenes which persisted for centuries and have only recently died out. These, drawn and engraved by Gaetano Zompini (1702–1778) in 1750 are (i) the fortune-teller, (ii) the Punch and Judy show, (iii) the rat-catcher and (iv) the seller of theatre-box keys.

Everything around me is praiseworthy,
a great, reputable work of joint human
endeavour, a splendid monument, not
of a master, but of a people.
GOETHE

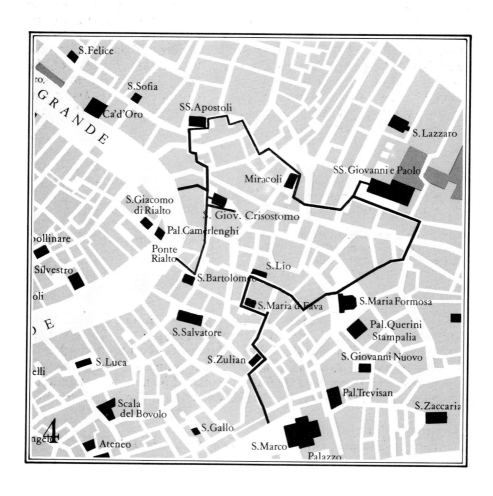

Walk 4

Querini Stampalia – San Zanipolo – Miracoli – Santi Apostoli

Start from the Piazza; go under the Clock Tower into the Merceria dell'Orologio. Immediately on the left is the Sotoportego del Cappello Nero. The white stone in the pavement commemorates the spot where a brick felled the standard-bearer of Bajamonte's rebellion. The old woman who threw it is represented in a relief on the sottoportico, crying 'Death to tyrants'. This sentiment is characteristic. The moral the Venetians drew from the overthrow of the Roman republic was that no individual should ever be permitted to acquire personal power. Even the power of the Doge was strictly circumscribed. In the context of the tyrannies and despotisms of mediaeval Europe, the diffusion of power achieved by the Venetian constitution was truly remarkable, and it was nowhere paralleled (outside primitive and tribal societies) until the rise of the modern democracies.

'Del mille trecento e diese
A mezzo el mese delle ceriese
Bagiamonte passò el ponte
E per esso fo fatto el consegio di diese'

In the year thirteen hundred and ten
In the middle of the month of the cherries
Bajamonte crossed the bridge
And because of that they made the Council of Ten.

Continue down the Merceria. Turn right into Ramo San Zulian, left at the church of San Zulian, diagonally across the Campiello San Zulian; the way narrows and soon the Piscina San Zulian goes off to the right. Go through the Piscina, over the bridge, and turn left under the Sotoportego Licini; then straight on through Corte Licini and Ramo Licini, to emerge in the campo and in front of the c18 church of Santa Maria della Fava.

First altar on right
G. B. Tiepolo: *St Anne, Infant Madonna and Attendant Angels*

Middle altar on left
Piazzetta: *St Anne, Infant Madonna and Attendant Angels*

Out of the entrance door, turn right and follow the wall of the church
(Ramo della Fava) for a few yards, turn left into the Calle de la Fava,
which emerges into a Campo (San Lio) – at which point, turn right into the
Salizzada San Lio. Along the salizzada for some little way, then left along
the Calle del Mondo Nuovo. This leads quickly to the Campo Santa Maria
Formosa. It has been used for bullfights and as an open-air theatre. In
this square is the church of the same name – mainly late c15 (extensively
restored, Italian government). At the foot of the Baroque campanile
(1611) – a grotesque masque. Of this hideous mask Ruskin wrote: 'In that
head is embodied the type of the evil spirit to which Venice was
abandoned in the fourth period of her decline, and it is well that we
should see and feel the full horror of it in this spot and know what
pestilence it was that came and breathed upon her beauty until it melted
away'; and Molmenti adds, 'rightly did Ruskin declare that human fancy
could fall no lower'. But this is simply an example of ignorance cloaked
under fine writing. The mask is not fanciful and it has a function.

It is a widespread belief that the Evil Eye can enter a building through the
doorway and that an amulet should be placed there. Hence the Jewish
menzuzah, the henna painted on the jambs and lintels of oriental houses, the
amuletic hand as a door-knocker and the devil mask seen in many western
countries; the last is on the same principle as the Medusa head which has for
millennia been used in Greece and Southern Italy as a protection. The more hideous
it is, the more efficiently it will act. And now for the second fact: the head over
the *campanile* entrance is not the product of a debased imagination or diseased
fancy. It is the accurate representation of a diseased model, one who suffered
from neurofibromatosis, or von Recklinghausen's disease, a rare, inborn malade.
LOWE

The entrance to the church is to the right – facing the canal

Architecturally this interior is unique. Rebuilt by Mauro Coducci in 1492 on an
earlier, probably eleventh century, plan, it is a peculiarly attractive cross between
the Veneto-Byzantine and the Venetian Renaissance styles, reminding one of
what the latter owed to the former. With its screens of slender columns
supporting the little cupolas and barrel vaults, the interior combines the
elegance of early renaissance ornament with the spatial effects of a Byzantine
church.
HONOUR

Santa Maria Formosa, grotesque mask.

Santa Maria Formosa was altered in the 17th, 18th and 19th centuries, bombed in World War I and extensively rebuilt in the 1920s, but although several features of the building as it now stands, such as the fully developed east end and the drum under the crossing dome, are not original, the church still retains much of its late 15th-century character.

The space of Santa Maria Formosa is impressively organized, and its wide pyramidal effect is unusual for Venetian churches.

The interior decoration of the building is extremely spare; there is not a single carved capital in the church. The 'entablature' of the nave and transepts is radically reduced to narrow mouldings. What amount to the architrave and cornice are done in Istrian stone but the high 'frieze' between them is just stuccoed wall.

It is characteristic of Venetian architecture of these years that there was little concern for the proportions of the orders; architects in Venice seem to have begun in a very different way from the Florentines. At San Lorenzo in Florence, for example . . . Brunelleschi's spatial effects were developed from the proportions of the orders; he began with a unit linked to the size of the columns and pilasters and then derived the plan and elevation from it. Codussi, on the other hand, began at Santa Maria Formosa with a particular combination of spaces in mind. These were organized in their own terms, and he did not care if it proved to be impossible to connect them all in a consistent and unified system of decoration; the pilasters and horizontal elements were stretched and shrunk to fit the space they had to fill.
LIEBERMAN

On the right, in the first chapel, on the altar (light)
Bartolemeo Vivarini: *Triptych*

In the s transept, on the left (i.e. the E) wall (light)
Palma il Vecchio: *Altarpiece – Saint Barbara*

An almost unique presentation of a hero-woman, standing in calm preparation for martyrdom, without the slightest air of pietism, yet with the expression of mind filled with serious conviction.
GEORGE ELIOT

The head is of a truly typical Venetian beauty; the whole is finished with the greatest power and knowledge of colour and modelling.
BURCKHARDT

The door at the end of the N transept opens out into the campo. The various styles of Venetian Palazzi are well represented around this square: No.5250, on the right, is a handsome c16 example (with a later superstructure). Fragments of Byzantine carving (including a cross admired by Ruskin) decorate No.5246.

Santa Maria Formosa in 1720, from the 'Gran Teatro di Venezia'.

Querini-Stampalia

The Querini-Stampalia Collection is nearby (summer opening 10.00–15.45 weekdays; Sunday 10.00–14.45; closed Monday). It can be regarded as an optional extra for the energetic. It gives an interesting impression of a late c18 Venetian aristocrat's house (less grand than the Ca' Rezzonico – p.155); the paintings are mainly of minor importance, but many have been recently cleaned and restored by IFM. It is reached by turning right after leaving the church: follow the wall of the church and cross the Campiello Santa Maria Formosa. The Gallery is on the second floor. Ring bell.

Room I
Scenes of c18 Venetian life

Room IV
Works by Palma il Giovane, notably (on wall of exit door, upper right) a *Desposition*.

Room VIII (Renaissance Room)
Giovanni Bellini (attr.): *Madonna and Child Blessing*
Giovanni Bellini: *Presentation in the Temple*
An early and unfinished work, closely modelled on a work of Mantegna. The additional head on the right may be a self-portrait.
Mantegna: *Presentation*
Palma il Vecchio: Portrait of *Francesco Querini* and *Wife* (unfinished)

Room XI
Longhi: *The Sagredo Family*

Rooms XI, XII and XIII
Works by Longhi, including (in Room XIII)
Longhi: *Duck Shooting on the Lagoon*
(so much better than the others, it is thought by Honour to be possibly the work of another artist)

Those omitting the Querini-Stampalia, turn left out of the church. From the campo take the opening by the clock – the Calle Longa. You will come to a bridge in front of you. Do not go over it; instead, go over the bridge on your left – the Ponte Tetta (from which are particularly charming views).

The way crosses over the Ponte dell'Ospedaleto and comes out opposite the Casa di Riposo – the Ospedaletto (almshouse). Inside ask to see the c17 oval staircase by Giuseppe Sardi, and on the first floor the Music Room – a pretty little c18 room with frescoes by Jacopo Guarana and Agostino Mengozzi.

This seldom-visited room is a complete piece of 'settecento' decoration, in which every available wall space has been frescoed and ornamented light-heartedly and intimately; only the existence of radiators there discreetly reveals that time has passed. The children of the Ospedaletto were famous for the concerts they gave, and Guarana has taken up the theme of music in a charmingly half-humorous, half-poetic Apollo with female musicians who play at one end of the oval room among painted marble columns. The whole deceptive architectual setting is the work of Agostino Mengozzi-Colonna, son of the architectural painter who had been Tiepolo's constant collaborator in such schemes. Agostino's 'trompe l'oeil' is in the best tradition of his father, while Guarana has peopled it with those vaguely classical figures in vaguely period costume, who are not taking themselves too seriously.

Part of Guarana's charm is in this unpretentiousness and even in irrelevance. The dog on the steps is sufficient to tell us that the fresco is Venetian: it has strayed out of ordinary life, to be teased by the woman at the right who extends a doughnut to it, and is a comic adjunct to Apollo earnestly conducting; and it also aids the illusionism of Mengozzi-Colonna's steps. Since Veronese, at least, there had been a cheerful Venetian tradition of irrelevance, if not irreverence in depictions of solemn scenes. Like his master Tiepolo, Guarana is not concerned with a serious classical world but with creating a piquant and impressive effect: which indeed he succeeds in doing. And Mengozzi-Colonna is concerned with creating an effect of space by a Palladian-style portico of double columns (almost like a miniature of Adam's portico for Osterley) and nothing but sky beyond. First the room is dignified by simulated architecture, its proportions enhanced by the figures, and then the wall is dissolved into the lilac space of limitless sky. Guarana and Mengozzi-Colonna thus assert, for almost the last time, that pre-occupation of their age with illusionism in decoration. . . .

LEVEY

The little curved singing gallery is characteristic of the period

The music, which, according to my taste, is far superior to that of the opera, and which has not its like, either in Italy or the rest of the world, is that of the 'scuole'. The 'scuole' are charitable institutions, founded for the education of young girls without means, who are subsequently portioned by the Republic either for marriage or for the cloister. Amongst the accomplishments cultivated in these young girls music holds the first place. Every Sunday, in the church of each of these 'scuole', during Vespers, motets are performed with full chorus and full orchestra, composed and conducted by the most famous Italian masters, executed in the latticed galleries by young girls only, all under twenty years of age. I cannot imagine anything so voluptuous, so touching as this music. The abundant art, the exquisite taste of the singing, the beauty of the voices, the correctness of the execution – everything in these delightful concerts contributes to produce an impression which is certainly not 'good style' but against which I doubt whether any man's heart is proof.

ROUSSEAU

Coming out of the Ospedaletto, Longhena's grand façade of the Ospedaletto church is immediately on the right. The porter of the Casa di Riposo will open the church (by Sardi and Longhena). Inside, an attractive c18 organ (restored, IRE); on the first altar on the N wall Palma il Giovane: *Annunciation*

On the opposite wall, in the panel over the fourth arch Tiepolo: *Sacrifice of Isaac*

A little farther begins the Campo San Zanipolo (Santi Giovanni e Paolo) – a good stop for coffee. You come first to a fine c16 well-head, and then to the late c15 equestrian statue of Colleoni, modelled by Verrocchio and cast by a Venetian caster. It was originally gilded.

When the great mercenary Colleoni died in 1484, he left his entire fortune of nearly half a million ducats to the State (which badly needed it) on condition that a statue was erected to him in 'the Piazza before St. Mark's'. The signory gratefully accepted the cash, but could not stomach the notion of a monument in the great Piazza, so reached a characteristic compromise with the truth. They commissioned the statue all right, and erected it in a piazza before St. Mark's – but it was the 'School' of St. Mark's, not the Basilica, and the memorial stands there still in the square outside the San Zanipolo.
MORRIS

The fine Renaissance façade of the Scuola di San Marco stretches from the canal to the church. It is thought that Codussi, who completed the top of the façade, intended to recall the curves of the basilica of San Marco.

San Zanipolo

The church (open 7.00–12.30; 15.30–19.30) was built by Dominican friars (cupola restoration, Italian government).

From the middle of the c13 the leading tendencies in all Continental countries were towards space in terms of uninterrupted breadth and plainness. These tendencies in Spain, Germany, Italy and France, were connected chiefly with the rise of the orders of friars, the Franciscans and Dominicans (or Grey Friars and Black Friars), founded in 1209 and 1215, and spreading from 1225 onwards.

The c13 churches of the friars were all large, simple and useful, with little to suggest a specifically ecclesiastical atmosphere. They did not need much in the way of eastern chapels, as many of the friars were not priests, but they could not do without very spacious naves to house the large congregations which came to listen to their popular sermons.

The friars, it is known, were the orders of the people. They scorned the secluded and leisurely existence of the other orders on their country estates, chose busy towns to settle in and there developed their sensational preaching technique as a medium of religious propaganda to a degree never attempted since the days of the Crusades. Thus all they needed was a large auditorium, a pulpit, and an altar.

Italy built the earliest of all Franciscan churches, S. Francesco in Assisi, begun in 1228, as a vaulted aisleless room with vaulted transept and a polygonal chancel. Later the Italian Franciscans and Dominicans have aisleless halls with timber roofs and Cistercian chancels or aisled flat-roofed, or aisled vaulted

The almshouse of Santi Giovanni e Paolo (San Zanipolo). The early eighteenth-century eye of the artist gives Longhena's somewhat heavy late Baroque façade a lighter, and more Rococo look.

building. (Saints Giovanni e Paolo, Venice, late c13; Frari, Venice, 1340.) But, whether aisled or unaisled, vaulted or unvaulted, each church is always one spatial unity, with piers (often round or polygonal) merely subdividing it. In this is shown a very important new principle. In early or High Gothic churches the nave and aisles were separate channels of parallel movements through space. Now the whole width and length of the room, thanks to the wide bays and thin supports, appears all one.
PEVSNER

The doorway of the church is late c15.

The paired columns supporting a broken entablature with a vine-pattern decoration derive from the Arch of the Sergii in Pula, which was also the source for the lower section of the Arsenale portal (see p.104) . . .
LIEBERMAN

In the arcades on the left side of the façade, the sarcophagus of the
Tiepolo Doges is another example of c13 Venice imitating the c6 (see
p.37).

On either side of the doorway, two reliefs – a c13 Byzantine
Annunciation; on the extreme right, a marble relief, very worn – *Daniel
in the Lion's Den* – perhaps c6. Inside, on the entrance wall, immediately
on the right – c15 monument to Doge Giovanni Mocenigo.

> Here the sad idea of death is completely banished, and the Christian
> remembrances are restricted in this representation, to *The Taking Down of
> Christ From the Cross*, to the *Savior* and to a few *Saints*, while the classical and
> pagan exaltation of life is emphasized and devoted to the glorifying of the deeds
> and of the figure of the valiant Doge. . . .
> LORENZETTI

After first altar on right
Bragadin Memorial

> The defence of Famagosta, the principal city in Cyprus, was one of the most
> heroic exploits of the age: the combined conduct and valour of the Venetian
> governor, Bragadino, were the theme of universal praise; honourable terms were
> to be granted to the garrison; and when he notified his intention to be in person
> the bearer of the keys, the Turkish commander replied in the most courteous and
> complimentary terms, that he should feel honoured and gratified by receiving
> them. Bragadino came, attended by the officers of his staff, dressed in his purple
> robes, and with a red umbrella, the sign of his rank, held over him. In the course
> of the ensuing interview the Pasha suddenly springing up, accused him of having
> put some Mussulman prisoners to death: the officers were dragged away and
> cut to pieces, whilst Bragadino was reserved for the worst outrages that
> vindictive cruelty could inflict. He was thrice made to bare his neck to the
> executioner, whose sword was thrice lifted as if about to strike: his ears were
> cut off; he was driven every morning for ten days, heavy laden with baskets of
> earth, to the batteries, and compelled to kiss the ground before the Pasha's
> pavilion as he passed. He was hoisted to the yard-arm of one of the ships and
> exposed to the derision of the sailors. Finally, he was carried to the square of
> Famagosta, stripped, chained to a stake on the public scaffold, and slowly
> flayed alive, while the Pasha looked on. His skin, stuffed with straw, was then
> mounted on a cow, paraded through the streets with the red umbrella over it,
> suspended at the bowsprit of the admiral's galley, and displayed as a trophy

---

*The church of San Zanipolo and its surroundings from the 'Gran Teatro di
Venezia'. At the time these two plates were published the square was not paved
save for a crosspath, the outline of which can be seen in the present paving.*

during the whole voyage to Constantinople. The skin was afterwards purchased
of the Pasha by the family of Bragadino, and deposited in an urn in the church of
Saints Giovanni e Paolo.
QUARTERLY REVIEW NO. 274

Second altar
Giovanni Bellini (? with others): Altarpiece in original frame – *Episodes
in the Life of St Vincent* in central panels and predella; *Annunciation* and
Pietà above (use light). An early work, its modelling plainly indebted to
Mantegna, but its colouring very much Bellini and Venetian.

> It survives in its original gilded frame, which has round arches and classical
> pilasters in the Renaissance style and was probably the first of its kind in Venice.
> The figures, which seem as if carved from wood, tower over low extended
> landscapes and both are again gloriously transfigured by light, so that its
> splendour becomes the image of their immaculacy.
>   The polyptych has a new unity, partly because the glances of all the figures are
> directed upwards towards the panel with God the Father, now alas lost, which
> originally topped the altarpiece, and partly because of the way Bellini organizes
> light and colour. Instead of adding one strong colour to another in the happy,
> disparate confusion of a Gothic polyptych, he balances the scenes against each
> other – two light scenes flanking a darker one in the lower tier, two dark ones
> beside a lighter scene above – and creates an ordered whole. The rapt and
> intense devotion of each figure is a variation on a theme common to the whole
> altarpiece, which has a formal and dramatic integration going beyond anything
> which had been produced in Venice before.
> STEER

In front of the entrance to the next chapel, on the floor – c15 tombstone;
just beyond, on the right wall, the Valier Mausoleum. This elaborate
Baroque sculpture (from the very beginning of the c18) did not, of course,
commend itself to Ruskin.

> Towering from the pavement to the vaulting of the church, behold a mass of
> marble, sixty or seventy feet in height, of mingled yellow and white, the yellow
> carved into the form of an enormous curtain, with the ropes, fringes, and tassels,
> sustained by cherubs; in front of which, in the now usual stage attitudes, advance
> the statues of the Doge Bertuccio Valier, his son, the Doge Silvester Valier, and
> his son's wife, Elizabeth. The statues of the Doges, though mean and Polonius-
> like, are partly redeemed by the ducal robes; but that of the Dogaressa is a
> consummation of grossness, vanity, and ugliness – the figure of a large and
> wrinkled woman, with elaborate curls in stiff projection round her face, covered
> from her shoulders to her feet with ruffs, furs, lace, jewels, and embroidery.
> Beneath and around are scattered virtues, Victories, Fames, Genii – the entire
> company of the monumental stage assembled, as before a drop-scene – executed

by various sculptors, and deserving attentive study as exhibiting every condition
of false taste and feeble conceptions. The Victory in the centre is particularly
interesting; the lion by which she is accompanied, springing on a dragon, has
been intended to look terrible, but the incapable sculptor could not conceive
any form of dreadfulness, could not even make the lion look angry. It looks only
lachrymose; – its uplifted forepaws, there being no spring nor motion in its body,
give it the appearance of a dog begging.
RUSKIN

After the Valier Mausoleum – still on the right, the early c18 chapel of
San Domenico. The curving canvas overhead is Piazzetta: *Glory of San
Domenico*, an early example of the aerial vision, a manner made famous
by Tiepolo. We owe the preservation of this painting (as well as other
restoration work in this church) to the American Committee to Rescue
Italian Art set up after the 1966 flood.

In the s transept: on the right (i.e. w) wall
Alvise Vivarini: *Jesus Bearing the Cross*

In the s wall, c15 window (restored VIP)

Below, on the right
Lotto: *Saint Anthony Giving Alms* (use light)

Under the saint, behind a parapet hung with a Turkey carpet, are two deacons,
in face and gesture so individualized and yet so typical that, in similar
circumstances, you still see their like anywhere in Italy. One of them receives
petitions and tries to control the crowd, while the other, with a look of compassion,
is taking money out of a bag to give to the poor, who hustle up, a dozen heads
producing the impression of a multitude. The deacon receiving the petitions is
one of Lotto's best figures, considered both as painting and as a psychology.
   The expression Titian gave to the ideals of his own age has that grandeur of
form, that monumental style of composition, that arresting force of colour,
which make the world recognize a work of art at once, and for ever acclaim it as
classic. But with all these qualities, Titian's painting is as untinged by
individuality as Bellini's. Indeed, to express the master passions of a majority
implies a power of impersonal feeling and vision and implies, too, a certain
happy insensibility – the very leaven of genius, perhaps.
   This insensibility, this impersonal grasp of the world about him Lotto
lacked. A constant wanderer over the face of Italy, he could not shut his eyes to
its ruin nor make a rush for a share of the spoils. The real Renaissance, with all
its blithe promise, seemed over and gone. Lotto, like many of his noble
countrymen, turned to religion for consolation. But not to official Christianity of
the past, nor to the stereotype Romanisms of the nearer future. His yearning
was for immediate communion with God, although true to his artistic
temperament, he did not reject forms made venerable by long use and sweet
associations.

Christianity, it will be remembered, owed its rapid growth and final triumph in large measure to the personal relation it attempted universally to establish between Man and God. Pushed into the background while the Church was devoting itself to the task of civilizing barbarian hordes, this ideal of a close relation between God and man revived with the revival of culture, and became in the sixteenth century the aim of all religious striving. A brave Italian band trusted that they would be able to make religion personal once more without becoming Protestant. We all know of the sad failure of Contarini and Sadolet. Lotto had the same temper of mind and he remained as unappreciated as they, for Titian and Tintoretto swept him into oblivion, as Carafa and Loyola effaced the protestantizing cardinals.

Italy was tired of turmoil and was ready to pay any price for fixed conditions and settled institutions. It soon appeared that the price demanded was abject submission to the decrees of the Council of Trent, and Italy paid it without scarcely a murmur. If the Council of Trent meant anything, it meant the eradication of every personal element from Christianity. Bearing this in mind, we can see how inevitable was the failure of men like Contarini, Sadolet and Lotto – men to whom their own souls were as important as Christianity itself, who wanted more personality rather than less. But Italy was not ready to see, that personality – as they wanted it – was a very different affair from the individualism of which she was heartily weary.

Both Titian and Lotto are dramatic. Titian attains his dramatic effects by a total subordination of individuality to the strict purpose of a severe architectonic whole. The bystanders are mere reflectors of the emotion which it is the purpose of the artist their presence should heighten; their personality is of no consequence. Lotto, on the other hand, attains his dramatic effect in the very opposite way. He makes us realize the full import of the event by the different feelings it inspires in people of different kinds.

BERENSON

High altar, on left wall, finely proportioned Renaissance monument – Memorial to Doge Andrea Vendramin. The marble effigy of the sleeping Doge nicely illustrates the Venetian concern with surface rather than structure: the back side is blank (a feature which, for Ruskin, epitomized the decadence of the Renaissance). On the right wall, c14 tomb of Doge Michele Morosini, on wall brackets, with canopy above – a typical Venetian design.

At the E end of the N wall is the entrance to the Chapel of the Rosary, on the ceiling of which are three paintings by Veronese: *Annunciation*, *Assumption*, and *Adoration of the Magi* (use light).

From the church, go out of the campo at the left corner, along the Fondamenta Dandolo, then over the Ponte Rosso. On the next bridge, a view of the Palazzo Van Axel; right immediately after this bridge, following the way to the left and emerging in front of the church of the

Miracoli (restored, not altogether successfully, 1970, by Stifterverband für die Deutsche Wissenschaft). The building is immediately charming. Part of the charm is in the surprise – the sudden approach, the un-Venetian style.

Miracoli

Santa Maria dei Miracoli, built by Pietro and Tullio Lombardo from 1481 to 1489, is the crowning work of the Lombard style. In bringing them to Venice they transposed the qualities of Milanese and Cremonese terra cotta into marble.[1] The colored areas are no longer merely decorative, but become basic elements of the spatial composition. . . .

Carpaccio . . . and Mansueti, faithful portrayers of the subtle charms of Venetian dwellings, often reproduced the luxurious effects of these many-colored inlays. The Lombardi used them profusely in their works and they are displayed to particular advantage on the pretty façade of the Palazzo Dario (1487).[2]

The altar screen is carved as delicately as lace, the cornice and pilasters are covered with graceful arabesques, and delightful bas-reliefs of putti and sirens ornament the base.

CHASTEL

Take the calle beside the church, over the Ponte Santa Maria Nova. On the left, the side wall of the Miracoli rises from the water. On the far side of the campo, turn left into the Calle del Spizier (following the direction to San Marco and San Giovanni Crisostomo and Rialto), cross the Campiello Bruno Crovato and turn right into the Campo San Canzian. Go over the bridge, cross the Campiello de la Casan; from the calle on the far side take the first turning to the left and cross the Campo drio la Chiesa diagonally into the Campo Santi Apostoli. The entrance to the church is on the right.

---

[1] The types of marble used are listed by Hare as Pavonazzetto, Broccatello Rosso, Veronese, Porphyry, Verde-Antico, Alabastro-pecotrella, and Serpentino.
[2] p.135.

Santa Maria dei Miracoli.

Santa Maria dei Miracoli built from 1481–89 to a design by Pietro Lombardo (1435–1515) who was also the architect of the nearby Franciscan monastèry which in this engraving by Luca Carlevaris was still connected to the church by an overhead gallery.

Santi Apostoli

After first altar on right
c15 Correr Family Chapel, attributed to Codussi, on the altar of which (plug in light)
G. B. Tiepolo: *Communion of Santa Lucia*
  From the church, we cross the campo towards the bridge. In front is the façade of the Veneto-Byzantine Palazzo Falier.

> The balcony is, of course, modern, and the series of windows has been of greater extent, once terminated by a pilaster on the left hand, as well as on the right, but the terminal arches have been walled up.
> RUSKIN

Cross the bridge, turn left and immediately right; go through the
Campiello Riccardo Selvatico and Calle Dolfin into the Campiello
Flaminio Corner and over the bridge on the left into Campo San Giovanni
Crisostomo. Just as you come into the campo, you will see the very
narrow Calle del Scaleter – which leads into the Campiello del Remer, on
the Grand Canal. The outside staircase and windows are vestiges of a c13
palazzo.

> One of the houses in the Corte del Remer is remarkable as having its great
> entrance on the first floor, attained by a bold flight of steps, sustained on four
> pointed arches wrought in brick. The rest of the aspect of the building is
> Byzantine, except only that the rich sculptures of its archivolt show in combats
> of animals, beneath the soffit, a beginning of the gothic fire and energy. The
> moulding of its plinth[1] is of a gothic profile, and the windows are pointed, not
> with a reversed curve, but in a pure straight gable, very curiously contrasted
> with the delicate bending of the pieces of marble armour cut for the shoulders
> of each arch. There is a two-lighted window on each side of the door, sustained
> in the centre by a basket-worked Byzantine capital: the mode of covering the
> brick archivolt with marble, both in the windows and doorway, is precisely like
> that of the true Byzantine palaces.
> RUSKIN

Return to the campo, for the church of San Giovanni Crisostomo. It was
built by Codussi about 1500 (choir ceiling c17). Its façade resembles that
of his San Michele in Isola (p. 188).

> The plan, a Greek cross with a central cupola was one particularly admired by
> Renaissance architects no less for its beautiful simplicity than its symbolism – a
> combination of the square and circle representing the relation between man and
> the universe and the cross standing for the redemption. There are two pictures of
> outstanding importance. Above the first altar on the right is Giovanni Bellini's
> *St. Jerome with St. Christopher and St. Augustine*,[1] painted in 1513 when he was
> an octogenarian. The treatment of the soulful St. Christopher and the gentle
> hilly landscape reveal how the old artist fell under the spell of Giorgione who had
> died three years before; while the elegant marble pilaster in the centre, which
> looks like the jamb of a chimney-piece, seems to have been taken from the work
> of another of his younger contemporaries, Tullio Lombardo. The influence of
> Giorgione marks, still more strongly, Sebastiano del Piombo's *St. John
> Chrysostom and Six Saints* on the high altar (1508–10). Indeed, the somewhat
> plump St. John the Baptist and St. Liberale who stands behind him were
> probably laid in by Giorgione himself shortly before his death. The third great

---

[1] Not there at time of writing.

The church of Santi Apostoli as it was in 1720. It was considerably remodelled later in the century (from the 'Gran Teatro di Venezia').

work of art in the church is the relief of *The Coronation of the Virgin*, over the second altar on the left, carved between 1500 and 1502 by Tullio Lombardo who also decorated the pilasters in the chapel. With its carefully modulated rhythm of draperies and its serious self-possessed figures, this strongly classicising relief was destined to exert great influence on Venetian painters, notably Bellini and Cima.

HONOUR

The *pala* which stands on one of the side-altars . . .[1] is dated 1513. The chapel is narrow and just deep enough to leave room for a small side-window. The artist has repeated this form in the arch and has used the natural light as lighting in the picture. So much has remained of the traditional definition of the place of the *Sacra Conversazione*. The arch is closed by a low parapet, similar to that of the chapel entrance, and is open above the parapet. Behind it there is a high pedestal of rocks on which St. Jerome, who has taken the Virgin's place, is seated. . . . The

[1] on the right.

attendant saints, St. Christopher and St. Louis, stand under the arch and before
the parapet. . . . Bellini [gives] . . . to the attendant figures the same full volumes as
in his *Pala di S. Giobbe* of the 1480s[2] they . . . look like piers supporting an arch;
even the forms within the semicircle are more plastic. However, on these convex
surfaces the artist freely displays the mastery of his brush and the richness of his
palette: faces, draperies, carved stone, rocks and tree – all are painted with the
same delicacy which you find in the Loredan bust in the National Gallery, and
have the same still-life quality; and this homogeneity of handling counterbalances
the plastic effect of the forms.
WILDE

Behind the church, a passage-way leads to the Corte Prima del Milion and
thence to the Corte Seconda del Milion, on the left of which is a Byzantine
archway with zodiac carvings of great beauty and assurance of style.

    We return to the church: the way to the left leads to the Rialto and San
Marco.

---

[1]Accademia, Room II, No.38 (p.74).   *Ca'd'Oro.*

We have rediscovered the great law of town planning which radiates so
delightfully through Venice.

The buildings people the sky: communications are precisely established, in
cardinal roads and piazzas, with canals at another level. The pedestrian is
master of the ground as he will be in the new town of our time.

LE CORBUSIER

Walk 5

San Rocco – Frari – San Pantaleone – Carmini – Angelo Raffaele – San Bastian – Ca'Rezzonico

Go first to the Accademia Bridge (vaporetto stop Accademia). The top of the bridge is a commanding position to view the Canal and its palazzi. Looking towards the Salute and reading the buildings from the right: first, a c18 palazzo washed ochre – the Palazzo Brandolin-Rota, where Browning stayed in 1878; next, a fine late c15 palazzo – the Palazzo Contarini-Polignac; farther away, towards the Salute, a one-storey white building – this is the unfinished Palazzo Venier dei Leoni, which now houses the Peggy Guggenheim Collection (p.94); farther away still, a red building, and then the Palazzo Dario. Looking the other way along the Canal, and reading the buildings from the left; first, the palazzo housing the British consulate, then a c17 palazzo washed dull yellow; then the fine early c17 Palazzo Contarini degli Scrigni; Longhena's Ca'Rezzonico closes the vista. On the opposite side of the Canal, looking left from the bridge there is a garden and beige-coloured building, and then the elegant c17 façade (topped by pinnacles) of the Palazzo Giustiniani-Lolin˙– an early work of Longhena.

We go over the bridge (away from the Accademia) into the Campo San Vidal: just beyond the campo is the church of San Vitale – now the Gallery of San Vidal (entrance on the left, at the foot of the campanile). The façade is a faithful restatement of Palladio's front for San Francesco della Vigna, p.107.

On the end wall of the chancel
Carpaccio: *San Vitale on Horseback* (the horse owing much to the bronze horses of San Marco) and over, *Four Saints, Madonna and Child.*

Emerging from the gallery we turn left and left again following the wall of the church and of the house built up against the church, over the Ponte de Ca'Vitturi, and straight ahead, until we can go no farther. This is the Calle dei Orbi: turn left here, and immediately right: we come out into the Salizzada di Ca'Malipiero, with the Grand Canal on the left (Campo San Samuele).

From here we get a good view of the façade of the Ca'Rezzonico immediately opposite: Longhena's design was carried out up to the *piano nobile* (first floor) in the c17 and makes use of the motifs from Sansovino's façade of the Library (p.43). The top floor was added in the mid c18.

To the right of the Rezzonico, two small palaces, then three mid c15 palaces all joined together, of which the first two are a 'double palace' – the Palazzo Giustinian. Wagner composed the first two acts of *Tristan* here.

As I was returning home late one night on the gloomy canal, the moon appeared suddenly and illuminated the marvellous palaces and the tall figure of my gondolier towering above the stern of the gondola, slowly moving his huge sweep. Suddenly he uttered a deep wail, not unlike the cry of an animal; the cry gradually gained in strength, and formed itself, after a long-drawn 'Oh!' into the simple musical exclamation 'Venezia!' This was followed by other sounds of which I have no distinct recollection, as I was so much moved at the time. Such were the impressions that to me appeared the most characteristic of Venice during my stay there, and they remained with me until the completion of the second act of *Tristan*, and possibly even suggested to me the long-drawn wail of the shepherd's horn at the beginning of the third act.
WAGNER

With our back to the Canal, we leave the campo on the left, and go down the Calle de le Carozze to the Piscina San Samuele, at which point we turn left and fork left down the Calle del Tragheto to the traghetto station.

On the opposite side of the Canal on the far left we see the Palazzo Foscari (the last of the three palaces joined together, which we saw from San Samuele). To the right of it, the Palazzo Balbi, topped by pinnacles, a late c16 building fore-shadowing the development of the Baroque; far to right, another pinnacled palazzo, built some two decades earlier – the Palazzo Papadopoli.

We take the traghetto to the other side. Looking back at the buildings lining the Canal, we can see on the far left the façade of the handsome mid c16 Palazzo Grimani, now the Court of Appeal, rising above the roof level of the other buildings. Nearer, we see the white façade of Codussi's Palazzo Corner-Spinelli, pre-figuring his later Palazzo Vendramin-Calergi (p.185). The last palace fully visible on the right is the Palazzo Contarini delle Figure.

In the intervals of the windows of the first story, certain shields and torches are attached, in the form of trophies, to the stems of two trees whose boughs have been cut off, and only one or two of their faded leaves left, scarcely observable, but delicately sculptured here and there, beneath the insertions of

the severed boughs. It is as if the workman had intended to leave us an image of
the expiring naturalism of the gothic school.
RUSKIN

To the left of it are four palaces joined together – the Case del Mocenigo,
in which Byron wrote *Beppo*.

I love the language, that soft bastard Latin
Which melts like kisses from a female mouth,
And sounds as if it should be writ on satin,
With syllables which breathe of the sweet South,
And gentle liquids gliding all so pat in,
That not a single accent seems uncouth,
Like our harsh northern whistling, grunting gutteral,
Which we're obliged to hiss, and spit and sputter all.

I like the women too (forgive my folly),
From the rich peasant cheek of ruddy bronze,
And large black eyes that flash on you a volley
Of rays that say a thousand things at once,
To the high Dama's brow, more melancholy,
But clear, and with a wild and liquid glance,
Heart on her lips, and soul within her eyes,
Soft as her clime, and sunny as her skies.
BYRON: *Beppo*

San Rocco

From the traghetto stop, follow the arrows marked Scuola di San Rocco.

The Scuola (restored, IFM. Open 9.00–13.00; 15.30–18.30) is a c16
building famous for its series of vast paintings by Tintoretto. (The
Annunciation on an easel beside the altar upstairs is by Titian.)

Tintoretto's adolescence fell in a period when Spain was rapidly making herself
mistress of Italy. The haunting sense of powers almost irresistible gave a
terrible fascination to Michaelangelo's works, which are swayed by that sense as
by a demonic presence. Tintoretto felt this fascination because he was in
sympathy with the spirit which took form in the colossal torsoes and limbs . . . .
Tintoretto had to an even greater degree the feeling that whatever existed
was for mankind and with reference to man. In his youth people were once more

turning to religion, and in Venice poetry was making its way more than it had previously done, not only because Venice had become the refuge of men of letters, but also because of the diffusion of printed books. Tintoretto took to the new feeling for religion and poetry as to his birthright. Yet whether classic fable or biblical episode were the subject of his art, Tintoretto coloured it with his feeling for the human life at the heart of the story. His sense of power did not express itself in colossal nudes so much as in the immense energy, in the glowing health of the figures he painted, and more still in his effects of light, which he rendered as if he had it in his hands to brighten or darken the heavens at will and subdue them to his own moods . . . .

It was a great mastery of light and shadow which enabled Tintoretto to put into his pictures all the poetry there was in his soul without once tempting us to think that he might have found better expression in words. The poetry which quickens most of his works in the Scuola di San Rocco is almost entirely a matter of light and colour. What is it but the light that changes the solitudes in which the Magdalen and St. Mary of Egypt are sitting,[1] into dreamlands seen by poets in their moments of happiest inspiration? What again but light and colour, the gloom and chill of evening, with the white-stoled figure standing resignedly before the judge, that give 'Christ before Pilate',[2] its sublime magic? What, again, but light, colour and the star-procession of cherubs that imbue the realism of the 'Annunciation'[3] with music which thrills us through and through? . . .

Christ and the Apostles, the Patriarchs and prophets, were the embodiment of living principles and of living ideals. Tintoretto felt this so vividly that he could not think of them otherwise than as people of his own kind, living under conditions easily intelligible to himself and his fellow-men. Indeed, the more intelligible and the more familiar the look and the garb and surroundings of biblical and saintly personages, the more would they drive home the principles and ideas they incarnated. So Tintoretto did not hesitate to turn every biblical episode into a picture of what the scene would look like had it taken place under his own eyes, nor to tinge it with his own mood.

BERENSON

The feeling for reality which made the great painters look upon a picture as the representation of a cubic content of atmosphere enveloping all the objects depicted, made them also consider the fact that the given quantity of atmosphere is sure to contain other objects than those the artist wants for his purpose. He is free to leave them out, of course, but in so far as he does, so far is he from producing an effect of reality. The eye does not see everything, but all the eye would naturally see along with the principal objects, must be painted, or the picture will not look true to life. This incorporation of small episodes running parallel with the subject rather than forming part of it, is one of the chief characteristics of modern as distinguished from ancient art. It is this which makes the Elizabethan drama so different from the Greek. It is this again which already separates the works of Duccio and Giotto from the plastic

---

[1]On either side of the altar, ground floor.   [2]Upstairs, small hall.   [3]Downstairs, entrance end.

arts of Antiquity. Painting lends itself willingly to the consideration of minor episodes, and for that reason is almost as well fitted to be in touch with modern life as the novel itself. Such a treatment saves a picture from looking prepared and cold, just as light and atmosphere save it from rigidity and crudeness.

No better illustration of this can be found among Italian masters than Tintoretto's 'Crucifixion' in the Scuola di San Rocco. The scene is a vast one, and although Christ is on the Cross, life does not stop. To most people gathered there, what takes place is no more than a common execution. Many of them are attending to it as to a tedious duty. Others work away at some menial task more or less connected with the Crucifixion, as unconcerned as cobblers humming over their last. Most of the people in the huge canvas are represented as no doubt they were in life, without much personal feeling about Christ. His own friends are painted with all their grief and despair, but the others are allowed to feel as they please.

BERENSON

Tintoret here, as in all other cases, penetrating into the root and deep places of his subject, despising all outward and bodily appearances of pain, and seeking for some means of expressing, not the rack of nerve or sinew, but the fainting of the deserted Son of God before His Eloï cry; and yet feeling himself utterly unequal to the expression of this by the countenance, has, on the other hand, filled his picture with such various and impetuous muscular exertion, that the body of the Crucified is, by comparison, in perfect repose, and, on the other, has cast the countenance altogether into shade. But the agony is told by this, and by this only: that though there yet remains a chasm of light on the mountain horizon, where the earthquake darkness closes upon the day, the broad and sunlight glory about the head of the Redeemer has become wan, *and of the colour of ashes.*

But the great painter felt he had something more to do yet. Not only that agony of the Crucified, but the tumult of the people, that rage which invoked His blood upon them and their children. Not only the brutality of the soldier, the apathy of the centurion, nor any other merely instrumental cause of the Divine suffering, but the fury of His own people, the noise against Him of those for whom He died, were to be set before the eye of the understanding, if the power of the picture was to be complete. This rage, be it remembered, was one of disappointed pride; and disappointment dated essentially from the time when, but five days before the King of Zion came, and was received with hosannahs, riding upon an ass, and a colt the foal of an ass. To this time, then it was necessary to divert the thought, for therein are found both the cause and the character, the excitement of, and the witness against, this madness of the people. In the shadow behind the cross, a man, riding on an ass's colt, looks back to the multitude while he points with a rod to the Christ crucified. The ass is feeding on the remnants of withered palm-leaves.

RUSKIN

To Tintoretto, lighting is the key to the emotional effect created by his pictures. We know from the early sources how much trouble he took with it, making small wax figures and disposing them in different attitudes under artificial light. And indeed the lighting with him seems almost always artificial or supernatural.

The lucid light of the Italian sun, such as Bellini and the young Titian had revelled in, says nothing to his tortured and agitated mentality which, like the Northern artists with whom he had so much in common spiritually, seems most at home in highly abnormal states of illumination, in magical, phosphorescent lights, lurid storms, in every sort of weird glimmer or forests lit by glow worms. Parallels between his art and that of the Middle Ages (which was already recalled in the work of some Mannerists) spring readily to mind, and of the medieval works easily accessible to Tintoretto, one in particular, the mosaics of S. Marco, may be relevant in this context.

They would have said little enough to the painters of the *quattrocento* and nothing at all to those of the High Renaissance, but it is in every way understandable that Tintoretto, with his romantic and anti-classical point of view, would have appreciated them. Whether or not it is legitimate to trace, as certain writers tried to do, actual formal influence from them in Tintoretto's pictures, it is at least very possible that the way in which their curved surfaces throw back occasional beams from candles with magical effect may have affected his highly peculiar lighting.

In the *Agony in the Garden*[1] there is a mysterious glimmer everywhere and other elements seem decidedly mediaeval in principle. For example, the foliage appears to be symbolic, or microcosmic: a few very large and very clearly defined leaves do duty for a whole hedge. Then again, in space composition Tintoretto is here more blatant in his disregard alike of classical prototype and even of physical possibility than ever before. Christ is suspended on no visible foundations and the mysterious procession of soldiers (violently juxtaposed in discordant scale with the Apostles) emerges from under the very ground where He sleeps. So symbolic and irrational a treatment of space had not been seen since the Middle Ages.

GOULD

The *Crucifixion* is to be found by going through the hall on the upper floor.

We are drawn into the *Crucifixion* by a range of phenomena: the chiaroscuro of its tonal structure and the meteorological turbulence of its setting, the openness of its spatial arena, the energies expended by the laboring figures, the palpable reality of recognizable portraits, the diversity of narrative incident, and, most centrally and significantly, by the pathos of the event itself. Yet, despite the fullness of our engagement, a certain dimension is, finally, absent here ... Tintoretto does not actually invite us to feel the vicious hostility of Christ's tormentors. We are convinced, rather, by signs of the mechanics of torture and by the apparent efficiency of these workers performing their assigned tasks; they participate in the great redemptive scheme with none of that perverse pleasure and with no awareness of the significance of their labors.

There is, in other words, a fundamental anonymity among Tintoretto's dramatis personae (and not only in the chorus) that is essential to his control of this panoramic spectacle. Each character submits to the dictates of the larger

[1] Upstairs, large hall, wall opposite stairs, second from right.

drama. There is little room for rhetorical display, as actions and postures, no matter how extreme or forced, fulfill explicit dramatic functions. In a painting so dependent upon gesture for its eloquence, the range of such acts is in fact surprisingly limited; if they are not completely passive, hands either work, indicate, or respond in awe. Even among the most immediate protagonists, the mourners at the foot of the cross, emotional response remains muted, restricted to expressions of pious concern and, at most, gestures of *admiratio*.
ROSAND

Frari

We turn right on leaving the Scuola and follow the wall of the church of the Frari (campanile and other features restored, I F M. Open 9.30–12.00; 4.30–18.00).

As we go round the corner of the church, we can see over the doorway (to the Correr Chapel) a c15 marble lunette: *Virgin with Child between Angels*. It has been brilliantly restored, with the help of British experts.

The church was built by the Franciscans. It is a large preaching church, mostly dating from the c14 (cf. San Zanipolo, p.120). We turn left inside the church. On the N side is the Pesaro Altar, on which
Titian: *Pesaro Madonna* (restored, Save Venice Inc)

On the left, behind the kneeling militant bishop Jacopo Pesaro, a harnessed warrior, his features probably those of Titian, has brought Turkish prisoners and raises his master's banner triumphantly. The impetus animating these figures is carried into the composition of the picture as a whole and supports the group around the Virgin. In this way the painter created here in 1519 to 1526 the first great example of a powerfully dynamic diagonal composition which was to become the prototype for Baroque painting as a whole.
DECKER

One's first encounter with the painting is from an angle . . . and the design itself is constructed to accommodate this oblique view. The vanishing point of the perspective construction lies beyond the frame of the picture to the left, indicating an ideal vantage point to the left rather than directly in front of the picture.

Because of its site, then, the *Pesaro Madonna* must function both as a wall painting, continually visible from a variety of angles as one passes down the nave, and as an altarpiece, to be approached frontally on a central axis when one worships at the Pesaro altar. As a wall painting, the asymmetry and obliquity of Titian's composition render it accessible from the left; the orientation of the steps to the Virgin's throne, reinforced by further architectural elements in Titian's first ideas for the painting, invites entrance from the side. The holy figures naturally follow this general arrangement. But the narrative sequence within the picture functions with respect to a frontal approach, the viewer facing the altar directly. The grouping of the Pesaro family – Jacopo Pesaro on the left, the others on the right – subtly modifies the obliquity of the spatial structure; the balance of the

two groups creates a certain centrality within the asymmetry of the design. Their profiled parallelism at first establishes a barrier at the level of the picture plane – the surface tension of which is broken only by the boy's face – but this simple tableau parallelism is only apparent. The situation is significantly complicated by the isolation of Jacopo Pesaro, whose location farther back in space than his relatives leaves open an area of pavement, a space which affords the first step into the painting from the oblique approach. Before the altar, however, our own immediate involvement in the painting follows a different direction, from right to left. Beginning with our encounter with the youngest Pesaro, we look to the left with his elders to the leader of the clan. Jacopo Pesaro, in turn, faces to the right, presented to the Virgin by his special patron, St. Peter; this is the main dramatic action in the painting, complemented on the right by the gesture of St. Francis, who presents the rest of the family to the Christ Child. St. Peter occupies the pivotal position in the design as the only figure on center; looking down and to the left while moving toward the Virgin at the right, he is the only one of the sainted figures completely open to the viewer. Out of this large-scale contrapposto of action, gesture, and glance emerges a self-contained dramatic situation which resolves the two different axial imperatives in a synthesizing composition of extraordinary balance – acknowledging all the while the validity of both.
ROSAND

It was almost unheard of to move the Holy Virgin out of the centre of the picture, and place the two administering saints – St. Francis, who is recognizable by the Stigmate, and St. Peter, who has deposited the key on the steps of the Virgin's throne – not symmetrically on each side, as Giovanni Bellini had done, but as active participants of a scene. In this altar-piece, Titian had to revive the tradition of donor's portraits, but did it in an entirely novel way. The picture was intended as a token of thanksgiving for a victory over the Turks by the Venetian nobleman Jacopo Pesaro, and Titian portrayed him kneeling before the Virgin while an armoured standard-bearer drags a Turkish prisoner behind him. St. Peter and the Virgin look down on him benignly while St. Francis, on the other side, draws the attention of the Christ-child to the other members of the Pesaro family, who are kneeling in the corners of the picture. The whole scene seems to take place in an open courtyard, with two giant columns which rise into the clouds where two little angels are engaged in playfully raising the Cross. Titian's contemporaries may well have been amazed at the audacity with which he had dared to upset the old-established rules of composition. They must have expected, at first, to find such a picture lopsided and unbalanced. Actually it is the opposite. The unexpected composition only serves to make it gay and lively without upsetting the harmony of it all. The main reason is the way in which Titian contrived to let light, air and colours unify the scene. The idea of letting a mere flag counterbalance the figure of the Holy Virgin would probably have shocked an earlier generation, but this flag in its rich warm colour, is such a stupendous piece of painting that the venture was a complete success.
GOMBRICH

The tomb on the other side of the entrance is that of Canova.

The Castel Forte at a canal crossing and the back of the Scuola di San Rocco.
The Scuola is a characteristic building of the second half of C16 (from the
'Gran Teatro di Venezia').

The ... tomb ... with its pyramidical superstructure and its suggestive half-open
door, was designed by Canova – not for himself, but for Titian, who had his own
plans for a truly Titianesque tomb, but died too soon to build it (he is buried in the
Frari anyway in the grandest mausoleum of all[1] erected 300 years after his death
by the Emperor of Austria, and surrounded by reliefs from his own works). In the
same church[2] the fine statue of St. Jerome by Alessandro Vittoria, with its
beautifully modelled veins and muscles, really portrays Titian in his old age.
MORRIS

Framing the entrance door, huge C17 monument to Doge Pesaro, with
caryatids.

In the middle of the church, fine choir: the work is almost entirely C15,
and has both Gothic and Renaissance elements. The arch of the choir
screen frames the high altar, carved almost half a century later and
taking its basic design from a Roman triumphal arch.

[1]Opposite Canova pyramid.   [2]Opposite the Pesaro altar.

On the high altar, the famous panel
Titian: *Assumption*
(restored, Italian government)

Everything has been said about the mighty painters, and it is of little importance
that a pilgrim the more has found them to his taste. 'Went this morning to the
Academy[1]; was very much pleased with Titian's Assumption'.

That honest phrase has doubtless been written in many a traveller's diary, and
was not indiscreet on the part of its author. But it appeals little to the general
reader, and we must moreover notoriously not expose our deepest feeling. Since
I have mentioned Titian's 'Assumption' I must say that there are some people
who have been less pleased with it than the observer we have just imagined. It is
one of the possible disappointments of Venice, and you may if you like take
advantage of your privilege of not caring for it.
HENRY JAMES

It expresses, first of all, the natural movement towards the altar as a centre
underlying the composition of all Gothic interiors. It is framed, a second time, by
the opening of the screen; and in the painting the swag of angels repeats the
arch of this opening reversed, thus completing the full circle. The figure of the
Virgin is an isolated, dominant silhouette: she is the patroness of this church.
But the composition also symbolizes the upward movement inherent in the
forms of all Gothic architecture. The Virgin is placed high above the apostles,
and the figure is, by her own force, moving upwards in a spiral. At the same time
this figure is the peak of a high and very steep pyramid, the base of which is the
central section of the group of the apostles. All gestures point upwards, as do the
Gothic windows. A further correspondence: the horizontal *caesura* coincides with
the division in the windows. Finally, the colour. The choir is built of red bricks
and is ornamented with yellowish ones. These are also the two main colours in
the picture. Thus the steep central pyramid is built up of three different reds:
rose, vermilion, and crimson, and is surmounted by the brownish-red mantle of
God the Father, while the Virgin is silhouetted against the golden-yellow halo of
air. Both above and below light comes, as it were, through the neighbouring
windows of the south side of the choir.
WILDE

In the *Assumption*, the group of Apostles, silhouetted against the sky, is created,
by strong cross illumination, from patches of light and shade. So strong is this
pattern that when our attention is not deliberately concentrated, the forms are
partly lost in it, and it is only by conscious effort that we attach the gesticulating
limbs to individual bodies. The grouping has some of the vital confusion of life
itself, and there are marvellous passages of direct observation, such as the hand
of the pointing figure in the background, half flattened against the sky, half
modelled by touches of light . . . .

---

[1] It used to be kept there.

The Frari Church and its Campo from the same source as the preceding illustration. The C14 campanile is unusual for its octagonal top.

In Titian, and in the Venetian school as a whole, this sensuous approach to visual data is matched by a comparable approach to paint itself. In order to record these effects, Titian immensely extends the possibilities of the oil medium which he is using, and, as a corollary, develops his feeling for the medium itself. A love of colour and texture in the thing seen has its natural complement in a similar love for the sensuous qualities of the medium in which it is recorded; and a feeling for paint, for the texture and surface of the canvas and the decorative pattern of the brush-strokes on it, is an essential element in Venetian art.

Venetian painting, then, is about colour, light, and space, and only secondarily about form. It can be called visual in a special sense, because colour and light and shade are, in fact, the raw materials of visual experience, and Venetian painters of the sixteenth century found the means of recording with paint the way in which we perceive them in the eye. They also found in oil-paint a medium of immense range and potentiality in which they could express their love of colour and texture for their own sakes. All these characteristics have their origins in an artistic tradition going back to Byzantium, and they continue as the main themes of Venetian art into the eighteenth century.
STEER

The inscription on the high altar of the Frari informs us that it was erected in 1516 at the charge of Fra Germano da Casale, prior of the Franciscan monastery. An unusual entry in the diaries of Marino Sanuto, rare for its explicit reference to a work of art, records the unveiling of Titian's picture two years later, on 19 May 1518. On that day Titian established a classical High Renaissance art in Venice, for in its dramatic gestures, its breadth of form, and its symbolically geometric structure, the *Assunta* ... epitomizes a style more commonly defined with reference to the art of Raphael. Critics since the sixteenth century have indeed marveled that Titian could have created a work of such monumentality before he made the pilgrimage to Rome. Venetian painting to that date offers nothing in the way of precedent and very little, even in the juvenilia of Titian himself, that can be said to anticipate the grandeur of the *Assunta*. The composition actually depicts the Coronation as well as the Assumption of the Virgin, and in interpreting the subject dramatically, Titian created a heroic figure type new to Venice. Abandoning the modest naturalism of his predecessors ..., he conceived the celestial realm as a truly supernatural phenomenon: the golden circle of heaven in the *Assunta*, like that of Raphael's *Disputa*, glows with a radiance beyond nature. In the art of Giovanni Bellini celestial light found expression through empirically comprehensible phenomena, manifesting itself as a purer distillation of natural light or as the reflection of golden mosaics.[1] ... Titian, however, depicted a divine radiance existing entirely on its own terms, a visual reality essentially different from that of this world. In this he realized, again like Raphael, new possiblities of expression and ideality.

ROSAND

On the left wall of the main chapel is the handsome late c15 monument to Doge Nicolo Tron. The chapel at the E end of the N wall – the Corner Chapel – has a wooden tabernacle on the altar, containing the triptych Bartolomeo Vivarini: *Saint Mark between Saints* (restored, Association France-Italie)

The chapel to the right of the main chapel contains the Altar of the Florentines: in the central niche of the altar piece Donatello: *John the Baptist* statue in painted wood (restored, Save Venice Inc). The original paint had been covered by a c19 restorer with a layer of thick neutral brown, and the inscription and date changed. The original date has been revealed as 1438 – when Donatello was in Florence.

In the next chapel on the right, and on the N wall – a funeral memorial.

An early fourteenth century or perhaps late thirteenth century tomb, an exquisite example of the perfect gothic form. It is a knight's; but there is no inscription upon it, and his name is unknown. It consists of a sarcophagus,

---

[1] cf the San Giobbe Altarpiece (p.74), or the triptych in the sacristy of this church, mentioned below – MG.

raised against the chapel wall, bearing the recumbent figure, protected by a simple canopy in the form of a pointed arch, pinnacled by the knight's crest; beneath which the shadowy space is painted dark blue and strewn with stars. The statue itself is rudely carved; but its lines, as seen from the intended distance, are both tender and masterly. The knight is laid in his mail, only the hands and face being bare. The hauberd and helmet are of chain-mail, the armour for the limbs of jointed steel; a tunic, fitting close to the breast, and marking the swell of it by the narrow embroidered lines, is worn over the mail; his dagger is at his right side; his long cross-belted sword, not seen by the spectator from below, at his feet. His feet rest on a hound (the hound being his crest), which looks up towards its master. The face is turned away from the spectator towards the depth of the arch; for there, just above the warrior's breast, is carved a small image of S. Joseph bearing the infant Christ, who looks down upon the resting figure; and to this image its countenance is turned. The appearance of the entire tomb is as if the warrior had seen the vision of Christ in his dying moments, and had fallen back peacefully upon his pillow, with his eyes still turned to it, and his hands clasped in prayer.

RUSKIN

In the last chapel on the right, on the altar
Bartolomeo Vivarini: *Madonna and Child with Saints* and (above) *Jesus on the Sarcophagus*

A door to the right leads into the sacristry, in the apse at the end of which
Giovanni Bellini: Triptych: *Madonna and Child with Saints*
Symmetrically about the axis of the picture are set the various figures – Saints Nicholas and Peter on the left and Benedict and Mark on the right, as well as the cherubs. Despite some remaining Byzantine influences (note the tapered hands of the Madonna), 'human sweetness and soft colour', as Fiocco remarks, expel the last traces of the Byzantine inflexibility which characterized the 'San Giobbe' Altarpiece (p.74).

The triptych still stands on the altar where it was erected, in the polygonal apse of the sacristy of the Frari, a small Gothic room of perfect proportions. The altar-frame, quite untouched, is the best remaining example of Renaissance wood-carving in Venice. It is perhaps not correct to speak of a frame in this case, for pictures and frame are inseparable; the altarpiece is one work, partly carved, partly painted, and its unity both in colour and design is complete. Like the tabernacle of the Pesaro altar, this tripartite whole corresponds to a classical form often used in Venetian architecture (for instance in monumental wall tombs); and it is equally true to say either that the figure composition produced this form or that it is homogeneous with this form. The steep pyramid of the central group reaches the cornice of the entablature; the two principal saints, Nicolas and Benedict, stand like broader piers between the pillars which enclose them. Above them the crowning motif of the candelabra and above the arch a high vase form a whole attic of ornaments to echo the structure. The picture

space does not appear to be detached from a façade of a different order of reality: the viewpoint is again that of the spectator – in the case of a small altar such as this, it is high enough for the floor to be seen – and it is taken at a considerable distance to avoid startling foreshortenings. Where a conspicuous perspective effect occurs, at the top centre, the gold of the carving is directly continued in the painted gold-mosaic of the barrel-vault and of the semi-cupola. As characters, these calm, contemplative saints are all members of the same family: St. Benedict is turned to the worshipper only to listen to his prayer attentively and to recommend it to the Child.
WILDE

A door at the opposite end of the sacristy leads to the chapter house, from which there is a view of the cloisters of the c17 building housing the state archives. Opposite the windows, a c14 monument with high relief depicting the death of the Virgin, and, over, the lunette of 1339 by Paolo Veneziano shows the Doge and Dogaressa being presented to the Virgin and Child.

We come out of the church into the campo. It is a convenient spot for coffee.

At this point, the energetic may make a small excursion. Take the bridge opposite the w door of the church; turn left, over the next bridge into Calle de la Chiesa which leads into the Campo San Stin; leave the campo at the far end and after a few yards turn right. On the left, we come to the courtyard of the Scuola di San Giovanni Evangelista (restored IFM). The IFM information centre is upstairs.

> ... a masterpiece of Venetian Renaissance architecture – an exquisite composition of grey and white marble, stone, brick and stucco, and as Ruskin remarked 'the most characteristic example in Venice of the architecture that Carpaccio, Cima and John Bellini loved'. Yet this apparently harmonious courtyard is in fact the work of several different periods and architects.
> HONOUR

The atrium is the work of Pietro Lombardo – who completed the Miracoli church (p.127) and worked on the choir in the Frari (p.141); the stunning interior staircase is by Mauro Codussi.

We return towards the Scuola San Rocco but, before reaching it, take the passage on the left, under the Sotoportego Campiello San Rocco, and continue over the bridge, under the next passageway, right and immediately left down the Calle San Pantalone. Before emerging into the next campo, it is worth turning left into the Campiello de Ca'Angaran. On the wall is a c9 or c10 Byzantine medallion, of an Eastern Emperor. Into the campo: the water ahead is the Rio Novo – the route of the 'direct' vaporetto to the station. On the other side of the water and on the left is a small palazzo, with a Byzantine horseshoe-shaped doorway (a rare example) on the ground floor and Gothic windows above. 'The very evident deterioration of this lovely palazzo' says the International Fund for Monuments, 'is a typical example of the damage being done to the irreplaceable architectural splendour of Venice.' Facing the water is the church of San Pantalone on the right.

San Pantaleone

The elaborate late c17 painted ceiling (restored, American Committee to Rescue Italian Art) foreshadows Tiepolo; it is reputed to be the world's largest painted canvas.

The second chapel on the right is the chapel of San Pantalone: behind the altar
Veronese: *San Pantalone Healing a Youth* (restored VIP)

In two or three altarpieces painted during the 'eighties (he died in 1588) Veronese shows real feeling and permits a deeper range of his emotions to enter his art than before. At the same time the colours become darker and the handling more summary. What seems to be happening is that he was at last becoming affected by the atmosphere of religious urgency to which other painters had been reaching for decades. Tintoretto's example, undoubtedly, had something to do with it and this raises a very interesting point. For in his youth, as has been mentioned, Veronese had toyed with the externals of Mannerism. Now he seems veering towards the more typically Venetian form which Tintoretto exemplified to an extreme degree . . .

The altarpiece of *S. Pantalone Healing a Youth* dates from 1587, the year before Veronese's death. Its effect as a whole is still far less fantastic than any altarpiece of Tintoretto. The scene is recognizably in a small back courtyard, the illumination is not mysterious – indeed, it is not stressed in any way – and the three main figures are clearly real – the group of the unconscious youth on the the left and the old man anxiously supporting him is in fact touchingly human. At the same time the figure of the Saint is imbued with more than human authority and dominates the picture spiritually and physically for reasons which are not at first apparent. The chief means, in fact, by which this is achieved would seem to lie in the strange liberties taken with the space composition. The low view-point excludes the Saint's feet, those of the old man, and those of the Page. The Saint towers over us, rising from no apparent source, and what we feel is his presence. Veronese has, in fact, denied the existence of space as Tintoretto did in his *Entombment*[1] and for the same reason. We cannot say exactly how this development would have shaped had Veronese been granted

---

[1] Accademia, Room X, No.217 (see p.83).

another ten years of life, but we may well believe that he might have ended his
strange career as a typical Counter-Reformation painter.
GOULD

Go to the Little Chapel of the Sacred Nail to the left of the chancel. On the
right of wall
Giovanni d'Alemagna and Antonio Vivarini: *Coronation of the Virgin*
(c15)

Scuola dei Carmini

Leaving the church, over the bridge, the way leads us into the Campo
Santa Margherita, at the far end of which is the late c17 Scuola dei
Carmini (restored, IFM) – the entrance on the right (open 9.00–12.00;
15.00–18.00; closed Sunday).

In the upper hall, in the middle of the ceiling
G. B. Tiepolo: *Madonna of Mount Carmel*

> . . . The scene which he specifically illustrates here was a vital moment in the
> history of the Carmelite order. The Virgin is said to have appeared on this
> occasion to S. Simon at Cambridge, though that detail has clearly not bothered
> Tiepolo. The scapular, two pieces of cloth joined by strings, is the means of
> obtaining an important indulgence according to a Papal Bull which is perhaps
> a forgery, but which Tiepolo accepts: those who have worn the scapular will be
> liberated from Purgatory through the Madonna's intercession on the first
> Saturday after their death 'or as soon as possible'.
>   The comforting doctrine of this statement is carefully expressed in the
> painting. Purgatory lies all about S. Simon, and the litter of tombstones, skulls,
> and cloudy horrors of yawning graves contrast with the tall white figure of the
> Madonna triumphantly wielding aloft the Child and swept through the sky by
> attendant angels. The vision is almost a hallucination, and the figures of it are
> heightened beyond normality. We feel, and share, the Saint's privilege as he
> crouches low before the air-borne apparitions; like him we seem annihilated
> before this infraction of Nature's order.
>   The picture certainly is part of belief, shared by Tiepolo no doubt as strongly
> as he shared belief in Christ's sufferings and Christ as Son of God. Indeed, so
> pleased were the confraternity by his work that he was made a member of it,
> and could thus partake of its posthumous advantages. The S. Alvise picture[1]
> presents a quite unmiraculous moment: when God was suffering as a man,
> unaided by his divinity. But Tiepolo's mind is instinctively on the side of divinity,
> excited by triumphs, apotheoses and glories; he magnifies the whole conception
> of the Carmelite vision to his own more splendid dimensions whereby Cambridge

[1] Visited on Walk 7, p.180.

sinks into being a Palladian-style cornice but heaven becomes a great space swept by agitated, graceful, feminine forms. In this world of celestial servants it is not the Madonna who holds the sacred scapular; the office is delegated to an angel who carries it in one hand while supporting the Madonna's draperies with another.
LEVEY

Chiesa dei Carmini

Out of the Scuola, the door into the c14 Chiesa dei Carmini faces you on the right. On the altar immediately on the left
Lotto: *Saint Nicholas of Bari* (use light)

What was Lotto's relation to Titian at this time? We have not a word in any contemporary writer or document to answer this question, but the *Carmini* altarpiece reveals clearly enough that *Lotto*, if not in personal relations with Titian, had at least studied his pictures, and been stung by them to emulation.

Whatever the nature of the contact, whether personal, as it scarcely could have helped being, or not, its result was the Carmini altarpiece, a work in which the qualities of composition and line, in which the conception and the feeling are to the highest degree characteristic of *Lotto*, himself, but wherein the vehicle and the colour-scheme tend to be Titianesque. The medium must have been – in so far as the present state[1] of the picture permits us to judge – a more fluid one and the colouring more what is called 'Venetian' – that is to say, ruddier, richer, and more fiery – than was usual with Lotto. Ludovico Dolce, a hack writer of some talent, and a parasite of the log-rolling company of which Titian, Sansovino, and Aretino were the chief partners, took occasion in his *'Dialogue on Painting'* to find fault with *Lotto's Carmini* altarpiece for its too fiery colouring. No-one today would be tempted to find fault with it on this score, and it is more than questionable whether such an objection could ever have been made in good faith. It is possible that Dolce's censure was nothing but an echo of Titian's fear of being equalled on his own ground.

Lotto's picture, far from being too fiery, does not attain the glow of Titian's masterpieces, but has instead a more than Titianesque subtlety in the juxtaposition and fusion of the colours. In few other works has Lotto created types so strong and beautiful, and seldom has his drawing been so firm, his modelling so plastic, and his colouring so glowing and harmonious. The landscape is one of the most captivating in Italian painting. The sweep of its outlines, the harmony of its colours, and the suggestiveness of its lights make an unwonted appeal to the imagination.
BERENSON

On the opposite wall on the second altar
Cima da Conegliano: *Nativity* (light on right)

---

[1] It was restored in 1953.

We leave by the w door. On the left (No.2613), c16 cloister. Cross the campo; turn left. At No.2596, the late c17 Palazzo Zenobio, now an Armenian college. Ask to see inside: pretty c18 loggia and spacious garden; upstairs, splendid c18 ballroom.

Continue along the fondamenta. Where it turns sharp left, we see – on the opposite bank – a c14 brick palazzo, the Palazzo Ariani. The intricate tracery of the *piano nobile* windows is made up of circles and quatrefoils, the basic unit of which (as Lauritzen has pointed out) is the central joint of a group of four of these units – a feature most easily grasped by looking first at the break in the pattern over the third window from the right.

Angelo Raffaele

Take the first bridge on the right (Ponte de la Maddalena) to the church of the Angelo Raffaele. (Entrance beside water on right.) On the organ parapet is a group of paintings by Francesco Guardi (1712–1793) which have also been attributed to his brother Gian Antonio (1698–1760). (Ask for light.)

There seem to be no 18th Century records of this series of small pictures *in situ*. They are not mentioned in the list drawn up in 1773 by the younger Zanetti (then Public Inspector of Pictures at Venice) of works of art at Angelo Raffaele; and this has suggested that they therefore date from after that year, so removing the possibility of Gian Antonio's authorship. It is hard to see why Zanetti did not mention them if they were in the church, unless he took them as merely part of the decoration of the organ case and too insignificant to need comment. If so, there is irony in the fact that he, who had lived long enough to see the complete evolution of the rococo style, did not glance at one of its final manifestations. In the Angelo Raffaele series there is the same extremeness as was appearing in France (possibly at the same time), in the work of Fragonard. The prettiness of them is almost a boudoir prettiness; the last vestiges of 17th Century solidity and prosaicism disappear and, beside Piazzetta, Guardi seems as incongruous as a butterfly against a bull.

If the series really dates from late in the century, this would make admirable sense as the last phase in Venice of that desire for air and light which Ricci had largely initiated. But the progress had never been logical or neat; and the Guardi perhaps adumbrated a final phase long before the calendar and historical neatness required. Yet from such an extreme, a return to order was inevitable. All over Europe the last exaggerated elegancies of the style were to be nipped by the colder and more correct standards of the neo-classic; everything that had been set in such quivering motion froze into marble attitudes, and beauty was sought in repose.
LEVEY

Canaletto, drawn by Antonio Zanetti.

(Cannalletto in Maschera)

At this point, there is an optional excursion to see the church of San Nicolò dei Mendicoli (restored, V I P): we take the bridge to the left of the w door, turn left and continue until we emerge outside the church San Nicolò dei Mendicoli. This is the second oldest church in Venice (after San Giacomo di Rialto, p.170); the late c16 painted wood statues are especially fine.

We return to Angelo Raffaele the way we came.

Those not taking this excursion should turn right outside the w door of the church of the Angelo Raffaele.

San Bastian

The campanile of San Sebastiano (San Bastian) is immediately visible. The church contains some fine works of Veronese, which are best seen in the order in which they were painted.

Last side-altar on left
Veronese: *Madonna and Child with Friar* – an early work

Sacristy (through door under the organ), a room with c16 panelling on the ceiling
Veronese (**1555**): *Coronation of the Virgin* (centre); *Evangelists* (in four surrounding panels)

Ceiling of the church
Veronese (**1556**): *Life of Esther* (Frescoes also by Veronese and studio)

High altar
Veronese (**1559–61**): *Madonna and Saints*

> A composition full of vigorous, spirited figures, in which the central ones are two young men leaving some splendid dwelling, on the steps of which stands the mother, pleading and remonstrating – a marvellous figure of an old woman with a bare neck.
> GEORGE ELIOT

The doors of the organ
Veronese (*c.*1561): *Presentation in the Temple* (outside); *Pool of Bethesda* (inside)

Chancel
Veronese (**1565**): *Scenes from the Life of Saint Sebastian*

Take the bridge outside the church; the Calle de l'Avogaria and Calle Longa lead straight to San Barnaba.

> On account of the cheapness of rents, this was the centre around which Venetian nobles collected who were ruined by extravagance in the eighteenth century, obtaining hence the name of Barnabotti. They claimed support from the State, and especial privileges of begging were accorded to their daughters; nevertheless they retained their votes at the Great Council, and sometimes sold them.
> HARE

Turn left into the campo, and left again. The canal on the right is crossed by the Ponte dei Pugni. From c14 to c18 this bridge – which had no balustrading in those days – was the scene of violent fights between rival factions, but the white footmarks were marks for wrestling.

Ca'Rezzonico

We go over the bridge and turn right, down the fondamenta to the Ca'Rezzonico (open 10.00–16.00 weekdays; 9.00–12.30 Sunday; closed Friday). We saw the façade from the Campo San Samuele – p.135. The restoration is not yet completed.

We go up the grand staircase, into the huge ballroom and then (through the door on the right) into the Room of the Allegory of Marriage – the G. B. Tiepolo fresco of the *Allegory* is on the ceiling. It is part of the wit of Tiepolo's rococo manner that the irrational suspension of his encumbered chariots should be almost, but not quite, convincing.

Go down the little staircase. On the right is the room dedicated to Browning, who died here. Go through the China Drawing Room and the Green Lacquer Drawing Room to the delightful Yellow Drawing Room in which
Longhi: *The Cup of Chocolate; The Lady's Toilet*

Back up the stairs, to the Pastels Room and thence to the Tapestries Room, with interesting furniture and three fine c17 Flemish tapestries depicting incidents in the lives of Solomon and the Queen of Sheba. In the next room – the Throne Room – on the ceiling
G. B. Tiepolo; *Merit, between Nobility and Virtue*

Cross the portego: on the other side, the room nearest the Canal is the Tiepolo Room; on the ceiling
G. B. Tiepolo: *Fortitude and Wisdom*

Pictures on the walls
Giandomenico Tiepolo: *4 Fanciful Heads of Old Men*

The rooms on the next floor are of a more intimate and domestic character. From the top of the stairs, the opening across the portego and somewhat to the right leads to the Guardi Room (three frescoes attributed to Francesco Guardi); out of this (continuing rightwards) we see the Alcove Room, with its c18 painted bed. Back through the Guardi Room, we come to the Green Lacquer Room, beyond which is the Longhi Room: it contains over thirty pictures by and after Longhi, among which
Longhi: *The Rhinoceros*

He records thus the various animals brought to Venice at carnival times, perhaps the most exciting of which was the rhinoceros which arrived for the carnival of 1751.

Its journey from Africa via Nuremberg to Venice is perhaps a symbol: something primitive and grotesque coming from that Continent so long thought of as productive of novelties, and being welcomed as 'a change'. There is an element of sadness and futility in the onlookers; the rhinoceros once seen, there remains no more entertainment to be extracted from it, and despite the gesticulating showman his crowd seem already to have exhausted their emotions of wonder and surprise.

Hogarth (Longhi has been compared to Hogarth) would have wrung something savagely satiric out of such a scene, sympathizing with the beast or with the onlookers. There would have been, in brief, a point to the picture above the mere record-making task of painting what the rhinoceros looked like. Goya (Longhi has been compared to Goya) would have seized like a bird of prey upon the very vacuity of the people he had to depict, enjoying their emptiness as a child enjoys the emptiness of a balloon: he could have blown it out to monstrous swollen proportions. Longhi no doubt had to tread more carefully at Venice, while at the same time his mind had shown neither desire nor ability to express anything other than what it registered as *seen*.
LEVEY

The eighteenth century had the strength which comes from great self-confidence and profound satisfaction with one's surroundings. It was so self-satisfied that it could not dream of striving to be much better than it was. Everything was just right; there seemed to be no great issues, no problems arising that human intelligence untrammelled by superstition could not instantly solve. Everybody was, therefore, in holiday mood, and the gaiety and frivolity of the century were of almost as much account as its politics and culture. There was no room for great distinctions. Hair-dressers and tailors found as much consideration as philosophers and statesmen at a lady's levee. People were delighted with their own occupations, their whole lives; and whatever people delight in, that they will have represented in art. The love for pictures was by no means dead in

Venice, and Longhi painted for the picture-loving Venetians their own lives
in all their ordinary domestic and fashionable phases. In the hairdressing
scenes we hear the gossip of the periwigged barber; in the dressmaking scenes,
the chatter of the maid: in the dancing school, the pleasant music of the violin.
There is no tragic note anywhere. Everybody dresses, dances, makes bows, takes
coffee, as if there was nothing else in the world that wanted doing. A tone of high
courtesy, of great refinement, coupled with all-pervading cheerfulness,
distinguishes Longhi's pictures from the works of Hogarth, at once so brutal and
so full of presage of change.
BERENSON

Across the portego, the room on the canal side contains two c18 pictures
Francesco Guardi (perhaps in collaboration with his brother Gian
Antonio) *Sala del Ridotto (Gaming Room)*; *Nun's Parlour*

The passage beyond leads through other rooms to reconstructed rooms of
the Tiepolo's country villa. A portico and passageway lead to the Portego
del Mondo Novo: a fresco on the ceiling
Giandomenico Tiepolo: *The Triumph of the Arts*

on the walls behind *Minuet at the Villa; Three People Promenading*

and on the largest wall
Giandomenico Tiepolo: *The New World*
The frescoes are surprisingly critical of the society they portray.
Giandomenico is generally described as 'charming' and 'amusing': this
notion is sharply modified by the dwarfs and hunchbacks of the next
room – the Room of the Clowns. The door to this room is on the right of
The New World.

Fresco on the ceiling
Giandomenico Tiepolo: *The Swing*

Frescoes on the walls
Giandomenico Tiepolo: *Tumblers, Clowns*

The top floor of the palazzo has china, costumes, a reconstructed
chemist's shop and marionette stage of the period.

In the 18th Century, Venice became the City of carnival. Everyone, Doge and
beggar alike, paraded in *bauta* and *tabarro,* and in a city once determined to
dominate the seas and extend its power and trade into every corner of the globe,
there was no longer thought for anything save amusement, perhaps to hide the
memory of the faded glory and lost prosperity. But the amusements themselves
were so gay, so charming, so tasteful, that pleasure-seekers from all over
Europe – gentlemen of leisure, financiers, noblemen and adventurers – flocked to
Venice to take part.
        The carnival opened, in fact, on the first Sunday in October and went on until
Lent, with a short interval from Christmas Day till Epiphany. In other words,

for six months every year the people abandoned their regular vocations, and, protected by the anonymity of the mask, threw themselves into the lighthearted pastimes which immediately became their main preoccupation. It was a charming, unreal way of life which the Venetians led during these six months when everyone did as they pleased, forgetting age and rank, but in time it grew to seem their only way of life. In other countries and earlier times, the carnival, like the Saturnalia of antiquity, represented a brief moment of licence and indulgence to every whim in defiance of customs and laws, it was, in other words, an orgy, and probably a useful safety valve; after a few days of mad debauch, people would return to their work in a decent and orderly manner.

In Venice, however, the carnival did not have the orgiastic elements which were found elsewhere – and which are still found today in places such as Basle, Cologne and Nice. It has retained an air of elegance and discretion, even in its excesses, and filled one half of the year so pleasantly that the other half was taken up with waiting for it to come round again. Then, as if touched by a magic wand, the town became a kind of fairy world, where all tasks were forgotten, all obligations neglected, and everyone enjoyed himself with unflagging zeal. If a piece of business was absolutely unavoidable, then only the minimum of time was expended on it. A solemn Senator would not wait even to leave the precincts of the Doge's Palace before donning his Pulcinella cloak, pulling its huge sleeves over his ceremonial attire and running down the broad staircase four at a time towards the gondola where a beautiful girl awaited him.

Behind the shelter of the mask, everyone did as he liked, mocking social convention, but remaining nonetheless within the bounds of taste and discretion. These required, for instance, that no-one should ever be recognised, even if his mask did not completely conceal his identity. 'Signora Maschera' was the correct form of address, admitting no distinction of age or profession.

The mask most usually worn by ladies and gentlemen of rank was an extraordinary white face, adorned with a huge nose shaped like the beak of a bird of prey, through which the wearer breathed. When we come across the mask today in museums or collections of old customs, there seems to be something disconcerting, frightening, almost ghostly about it. For the 18th Century Venetians, however, it had the advantage of covering the face completely. Furthermore, it was always worn with a long black cloak which hid the entire body.

A crowd dressed uniformly in black and masked in chalky white would have looked doleful and funereal, but fortunately gayer disguises were also to be found in fantastic shapes and gaudy colours. One of the most popular was Pulcinella, who wore a tall white conical hat, a wide tunic, huge trousers, and a colossal nose. This mask had a long history; it existed in Roman times, and it may even have been worn by the Etruscans. Pulcinella is a clown, but a grotesque and sinister clown, strangely bound up with legends of death and sexuality; his tremendous nose is a phallic symbol. Usually Pulcinellas went about in groups, indulging in all kinds of pranks. By tradition they were gluttonous, stuffing themselves whenever possible at other people's expense. They shouted obscene jokes, and, all dressed in white as they were, they seemed like noisy lewd ghosts.

BRION

The vaporetto can take us back to San Marco.

Sketch notes made by Canaletto, c.1733, and Turner, 1819. Canaletto's colour notations are clearly marked on the façade, side walls and flanking palaces of the Palazzo Grimani. In 1819 Turner incorrectly identifies the campanile of San Samuele (on the right) as Santo Stefano; the Ca' Rezzonico is clearly drawn on the left, but not marked.

It is possible to dislike Venice, and to entertain the sentiment in a responsible and intelligent manner. There are travellers who think the place odious, and those who are not of this opinion often find themselves wishing that the others were only more numerous. The sentimental tourist's sole quarrel with his Venice is that he has too many competitors there. He likes to be alone; to be original; to have (to himself, at least) the air of making discoveries. The Venice of today is a vast museum where the little wicket that admits you is perpetually turning and creaking, and you march through the institution with a herd of fellow-gazers. There is nothing left to discover or describe, and originality of attitude is completely impossible.

HENRY JAMES

Walk 6

Santo Stefano – Rialto – San Cassiano – Ca'd'Oro

Leave the Piazza at the bottom end (with your back to San Marco, at the far left-hand corner) and follow the way until it opens out into a campo. This is the Campo San Moisè: it has a church (Saint Moses) with a heavy c17 façade. It does not merit a visit, but has one curiosity.

> The Church contains, near the entrance, the grave of Law, the originator of the South Sea Bubble, who died here, 1729. Montesquieu, who met him at Venice, wrote: "C'était le même homme, toujours l'esprit occupé de projets, toujours la tête remplie de calculs et de valeurs numéraires ou représentatives. Il jouait souvent, et assez gros jeu, quoique sa fortune fut fort mince."
> HARE

The Venetians adopted the Byzantine canonizations of old testament heroes: this is the church of Saint Moses; others were dedicated to Saint Job (San Giobbe), Saint Samuel (p.135) and Saint Jeremiah (p.177).

Over the bridge, we enter the Calle Larga XXII Marzo: the name celebrates the day in 1848 when the Venetians under Daniel Manin rebelled – unsuccessfully in the end— against the Austrians.

Down the Calle Larga XXII Marzo (note for future reference, on the right, the entrance to Calle delle Veste, which leads to the Fenice Theatre), follow the way into the Campo Santa Maria Zobenigo. Leading off from the far left corner of the campo is the Calle del Dose (Doge) which brings us down to the Canal: the Fondamenta San Maurizio gives a good view of Santa Maria della Salute (left). To the right of the church you can see the canal façade of the Abbey of San Gregorio: the c14 doorway, the relief above it, and the trilobate arch windows on either side of it remain from an old abbey.

On the right, the white, single-storey building is the Palazzo Venier dei Leoni, which houses the Peggy Guggenheim Collection (p.94); to the left of it, an ochre building, then the late c15 façade of the Palazzo Dario. Behind us, at the far end of the campo is the church of Santa Maria Zobenigo: the splendid c17 façade is in the full Venetian Baroque manner, a display in praise of the founder and his family and unrelated to any religion.

The fabric, the organ and the pictures have been excellently restored by
I F M.

In the chapel on the s side, small marble-framed panel; on the right wall
immediately on entering
Vittoria: Portrait (c16)

On the far wall of the chapel itself
P. P. Rubens (partly): *Madonna with Child and St John*

In the choir, on the N and s walls, next to the windows, two organ shutters
Tintoretto: *St Luke and St Matthew* (N)
Tintoretto: *St John and St Mark* (s)

Outside the church we see the stump of the campanile (collapsed, 1774).
Follow the way, over the Ponte de la Feltrina and the Ponte de
Ca'Zagari, to the Campo San Maurizio. Cross the campo to the Calle del
Piovan. Immediately on the right (No.2762) is a small early c16 building
with reliefs.

> One of the shops, no. 2266,[1] is the agent for the Fortuny silks so highly praised
> by Proust. They are made in a factory of the Giudecca and frequently repeat the
> patterns of textiles in paintings by Veronese and Tiepolo.
> HONOUR

The way continues to the Ponte San Maurizio: looking right from the
bridge, we can see that the water goes under the church of Santo Stefano.
Over the bridge, we come into the Campo Santo Stefano – illustrated
opposite. In the far corner on your left you will find a small campo,
dominated by the Palazzo Pisani (now the Music Conservatory) – begun
in the late c16 and completed in the c18. The courtyards are delightfully
separated by open loggias on the upper floors.

Santo Stefano

At the other end of the campo is the church of Santo Stefano (restored,
Comitato Italiano per Venezia). We pass on the right a pair of identical
buildings – unusually separated by a calle.

---

[1] When Hare was writing, the shop was in the Calle Larga X X I I Marzo.

One of the largest and busiest of Venetian squares, the Campo Santo Stefano was until the earliest years of C19 the scene of bear baiting and bull fighting (from the 'Gran Teatro di Venezia').

The church has an attractive Gothic doorway (c15); the long nave is flanked by columns of thin ogival arches; the roof is in 'ship's keel' form. Its chief glory, as Sir Ashley Clarke puts it, is in the polychrome effect of the altars, columns, capitals and *intarsia* made of many different kinds of marble.

A door at the end of the right aisle leads into the sacristy (light on entrance wall).

On the right wall (right to left)
Tintoretto: *Washing of the Feet*; *The Last Supper*; *Jesus in the Garden*

The fast food café outside the church was formerly a 'scuola' – a small c15 relief remains on the wall. Turn right and follow the way to the top of the Ponte dei Frati: immediately on the right, through the door, is a glimpse of a c17 convent cloister. In the campo – Campo Sant' Anzolo (Angelo) – on the left, a tiny c12 oratory, recently restored. Behind us we can see the leaning campanile of Santo Stefano. On the right side of the campo, next to the red-coloured building – a fine c15 pointed-arch façade; on the other side of the campo is another c15 pointed-arch façade, and on the left of it a rather severe c17 façade.

Out of the campo, the way continues down the Calle de la Mandola and over the Ponte de la Cortesia into the Campo Manin, with a statue of Daniele Manin in the middle. Turn right out of the campo, take the Calle de la Vida – it turns left, and an archway on the right leads to a courtyard from which one can see the spiral staircase (restored, IFM) of the Palazzo Contarini del Bovolo (c.1499) – illustrated opposite and on half title.

Turn right on re-entering the campo, and follow the way, through the Rio terrà San Paternian into the Campo San Luca; take the middle left way out of the campo (the Calle del Forno) and follow the way through the Calle del Teatro to the Campo San Salvador. The church is immediately on the right: it is a c16 building, with a mainly c17 façade – illustrated on p.167.

> The interior (reached by a high flight of steps with the ancient crypt beneath) is one of the finest examples of late Renaissance architecture in Venice and forecasting the classical style, with its spaciousness, severity of line and solid yet graceful construction . . . .
> LORENZETTI

Third altar on the right
Titian: *Annunciation*
The picture is very dark. It is signed *fecit fecit* – some say to emphasize the miracle of his activity, some say to impress upon his monastic patrons the authenticity of the picture.

Beneath a circular glass panel, in front of the high altar
Four c16 frescoes by Francesco Titian: *Scenes in the life of Jesus*

On the high altar
Titian: *Transfiguration*

> It is as impossible to keep untouched by what happens to your neighbours as to have a bright sky over your own house when it is stormy everywhere else. Spain did not directly dominate Venice, but the new fashions of life and thought inaugurated by her nearly universal triumph could not be kept out. It brought home to all Italians, even to the Venetians, the sense of the individual's helplessness before organized power – a sense which, as we have seen, the early Renaissance, with its belief in the omnipotence of the individual, totally lacked. This was not without a decided influence on art. In the last three decades of his long career, Titian did not paint man as if he were as free from care and as fitted

Giovanni Castellozzi drew the staircase of the Palazzo Contarini del Bovolo ('snailshell' in Venetian) in 1721. Reached by a small alleyway off the Campo Manin, this courtyard is one of Venice's most famous 'secret' places.

to his environment as a lark on an April morning. Rather did he represent man
as acting on his environment and suffering from its reactions. He made the faces
and figures show clearly what life had done to them.
BERENSON

Chapel in the left apse
Giovanni Bellini: *Supper at Emmaus*

Right outside the church, down the Marzarieta 2 Aprile (on 2 April 1849
the Venetians proclaimed resistance to the Austrians 'at all costs'); to the
Campo San Bartolomeo. In the middle of the campo there is the
monument to Carlo Goldoni.

Goldoni – good, gay, sunniest of souls –
Glassing half Venice in that verse of thine –
What though it just reflect the shade and shine
Of common life, nor render, as it rolls,
Grandeur and gloom? Sufficient for the shoals
Was Carnival: Parini's depths enshrine
Secrets unsuited to that opaline
Surface of things which laughs along thy scrolls.
There throng the people: how they come and go,
Lisp the soft language, flaunt the bright garb, – see, –
On Piazza, Calle, under Portico
And over Bridge! Dear king of Comedy,
Be honoured! Thou that did'st love Venice so,
Venice, and we who love her, all love thee.
BROWNING

On the right is a house through which a sottoportico passes.

The house faces the bridge, and its second storey has been built in the 13th
Century, above a still earlier Byzantine cornice remaining, or perhaps
introduced from some other ruined edifice, in the walls of the first floor. The
windows of the second storey . . . have capitals constantly varying in the form of
the flower or leaf introduced between their volutes.
RUSKIN

Rialto

The salizzada to the left leads to the Rialto Bridge (restored, Venezia
Nostra; illustrated on pp. 169 and 171). As Hare notes, the Rialto, which
Shakespeare alludes to when Shylock is made to say,

A mid C17 façade in the grand manner by Giuseppe Sardi fronts the C16 church of San Salvatore. The original was the combined work of several earlier architects. On the right is the Scuola di San Teodore with its fine C17 façade, also the work of Sardi, subsequently to become a cinema (from the 'Gran Teatro di Venezia').

"Signor Antonio, many a time and oft
In the Rialto you have rated me
About my monies" –

refers, of course, to this quarter of the town and not to the bridge.

There have been several bridges on this site. The first was a bridge of boats. The second was broken during the Tiepolo revolution in 1310, when the rebels fled across the canal. The third collapsed in 1444 during the Marchioness of Ferrara's wedding procession. The fifth, portrayed in Carpaccio's picture,[1] had a drawbridge in the middle. It was temporarily removed in 1452 to let the King of Hungary pass by in suitable state with the Duke of Austria; and it became so rickety over the years that one chronicler described it as 'all gnawed, and suspended in the air as if by a miracle'. The sixth was the subject of a famous

[1] Accademia, Room XX, No.566 (p.89).

sixteenth-century architectural competition. Sansovino, Palladio, Scamozzi, Fra Giocondo and even Michelangelo all submitted designs (you may see Michelangelo's, I am told, at the Casa Buonarroti in Florence). Most of the competitors suggested multi-arched bridges, but one, Antonio da Ponte, boldly proposed a single high arch, based upon 12,000 stakes, with a span of more than 90 feet, a height of 24, and a width of 72. This was a daring gesture. Da Ponte was official architect to the Republic, and the Signory was hardly lenient with employees' errors – Sansovino himself was shortly to be imprisoned when his new library building unfortunately fell down. Nevertheless da Ponte's design was accepted, and the bridge was built in two years. It has been a subject of controversy ever since. Many Venetians disliked it at the time, or mocked it as an unreliable white elephant; many others objected when its clean arch was loaded with the present picturesque superstructure of shops; and it has been, until recently, fashionable to decry it as lumpish and unworthy (though several great painters have fondly pictured it, including Turner in a lost canvas).

Structurally, it was a complete success – during rioting in 1797 they even fired cannon from its steps, to dispel the mobs: and for myself, I would not change a stone of it. I love the quaint old figures of St. Mark and St. Theodore on the station side of the bridge. I love the Annunciation on the other side, angel at one end, Virgin at the other, Holy Ghost serenely aloft in the middle. I love the queer whale-back of the bridge, humped above the markets, and its cramped little shops, facing resolutely inwards. I think one of the great moments of the Grand Canal occurs when you swing round the bend beside the fish market and see the Rialto there before you, precisely as you have imagined it all your life, one of the household images of the world, and one of the few Venetian monuments to possess the quality of geniality.
MORRIS

The Canal embodies part of the course of the River Brenta through the Lagoon: 'up' the Canal is towards the station, on our right; 'down' the Canal is towards San Marco, on our left. We climb the bridge to the summit. Looking down the Canal from the left side of the bridge, we can see, just over the pontoon of the ferry station, a handsome façade of the c16. It is Sansovino's Palazzo Dolfin-Manin, now housing the Banca

---

The Rialto Bridge. The segmental arch bridge known in China since C7 did not appear in Europe until after the return of Marco Polo, and then it was in the form of the Ponte Vecchio in Florence. Da Ponte's design was obviously based on the earlier model. Michelangelo (to whom the design is wrongly attributed in Israel Sylvestri's engraving of 1661), Sansovino, Palladio and Scamozzi all produced plans which were never adopted. The illustration (below) shows the west side and is a nearly identical view as in the earlier print (top). The Palazzo Camerlenghi occupies the centre of the upper right picture to the right of the east side of the bridge and can be seen in these and the two following pictures (all from the 'Gran Teatro di Venezia').

Veuë du pont de Realte de Venize jnuenté par Michel Ange.

Grané par Ifrael fculfsbre.   P.Mariette ex. Auec priuil. du Roy.

d'Italia. To the right of it, the reddish-coloured c15 palazzo in Venetian
Gothic style is the Palazzo Bembo. Hare remarks on the 'beautiful
Byzantine cornice above the entresol'. Farther away, on the same side of
the canal, the tallest building is the fine c16 Palazzo Grimani (p.159).

Up the Canal, we can see, close by on the right, the Fondaco dei
Tedeschi, basically an early c15 warehouse for German merchants (and
formerly frescoed by Titian and Giorgione) but modified in the last
century and restored in this. It is now the General Post Office. On the left
is the early c16 Palazzo dei Camerlenghi. The handsome detailing of this
palazzo can be seen at close quarters as we go down the steps.

Over the bridge and along the Ruga dei Oresi we come soon to the
entrance (on the right) to the church of San Giacomo di Rialto: It is an
c11 structure and part of the original material remains – see the capitals
supporting the vaulted ceiling.

We leave the church by the w door: the colonnaded buildings are early
c16. The façade of the church was restored in the c17. The Gothic portico
is the only remaining one of its kind in Venice. Opposite is the Porticato
del Banco Giro. (The name comes from the Banco Giro, a circulating
credit bank, established here in the c12). At the foot of the fourth pillar
from the left you find the proclamation stone called Gobbo di Rialto
(hunchback of Rialto) from the c16 statue. The other proclamation stone
stands by the façade of San Marco.

Continue along the Ruga dei Oresi and the Ruga dei Spezier into the
Campo de le Becarie. On the right is the Fish Market (built 1907).

Of all the spectacular food markets in Italy the one near the Rialto in Venice
must be the most remarkable. The light of a Venetian dawn in early summer –
you must be about at four o'clock in the morning[1] to see the market coming to
life – is so limpid and so still that it makes every separate vegetable and fruit
and fish luminous with a life of its own, with unnaturally heightened colours
and clear stencilled outlines. Here the cabbages are cobalt blue, the beetroots
deep rose, the lettuces clear pure green, sharp as glass. Bunches of gaudy gold
marrow-flowers show off the elegance of pink and white marbled bean pods,
primrose potatoes, green plums, green peas. The colours of the peaches, cherries
and apricots, packed in boxes lined with sugar-bag blue paper matching the
blue canvas trousers worn by the men unloading the gondolas, are reflected in
the rose-red mullet and the orange *vongole* and *canestrelle* which have been
prised out of their shells and heaped into baskets. In other markets, on other
shores, the unfamiliar fishes may be vivid, mysterious, repellent, fascinating,
and bright with splendid colour; only in Venice do they look good enough to eat.
In Venice even ordinary sole and ugly great skate are striped with delicate lilac
lights, the sardines shine like newly-minted silver coins, pink Venetian *scampi*
are fat and fresh, infinitely enticing in the early dawn.

---

[1] I have found this time too early.

As Lieberman observes, the Palazzo dei Camerlenghi is unusual in that it is free-standing and decorated equally on all sides. The decorative style harks back to the E wing courtyard of the Ducal Palace (p.49), designed nearly forty years earlier.

The gentle swaying of the laden gondolas, the movements of the market men as they unload, swinging the boxes and baskets ashore, the robust life and rattling noise contrasted with the fragile taffeta colours and the opal sky of Venice – the whole scene is out of some marvellous unheard-of ballet.
ELIZABETH DAVID

San Cassiano

Leave the campo by the bridge (Ponte de le Becarie), under the sotto-portico, turning left after the next sottoportico; take the next calle on the right (Calle de l'Erbarol), then left into the Campo San Cassan. The church of San Cassiano faces the water.

To the left of the high altar
Tintoretto: *Crucifixion*

The Crucifixion is [one of the finest Tintorets] in Europe . . . . The horizon is so low, that the spectator must fancy himself lying at full length on the grass, or rather among the brambles and luxuriant weeds, of which the foreground is entirely composed. Among these the seamless robe of Christ has fallen at the foot of the Cross; the rambling briars and wild grapes thrown here and there over its folds of rich but pale crimson.
RUSKIN

The little c18 chapel Del Medico San Carlo – entered by a gate in the N wall – has been restored by the Association France-Italie. To leave the campo we go back behind the church: then through the Calle del Campaniel to the Canal, walk along the Canal to the arched building – the Fish Market – and take the traghetto to the other side of the Canal. As you do so, look across the Canal and a little to the right: you will see a modest palazzo (the Ca'da Mosto) with a round-arch arcade at water level – one of the few remaining examples of c13 Veneto-Byzantine style.

Rising from the Canal just to the left of the landing-stage is the splendid façade (restored, I F M) of the Ca'd'Oro.

We land in the Campo Santa Sofia. At the far end of the campo, turn left and left again. The entrance to the Galleria Giorgio Franchetti, in the Ca'd'Oro (open 9.00–14.00 Tuesday to Saturday; 9.00–13.00 Sunday and public holidays; closed Monday) is on the right.

Ca'd'Oro

One can no longer enter the upper floors by the external staircase: this can be seen by going through the glass doors at the far end of the entrance hall. The courtyard is characteristic: an open-air staircase (formerly with wooden roof) early c15 well-head in red marble. Along the walls – busts, statues, altars, columns – mostly Roman copies of Greek works.

The c15 building has been extensively restored. We may begin by going straight up to the loggia, from which there is a fine view of the Canal. On the walls there are some interesting Byzantine and Veneto-Byzantine carvings (further examples are at the far end of the portego). In the room at the far end of the loggia are photographs taken during the work of restoration.

Returning through the glass doors, we find on the left three rooms containing a collection of bronzes.

> The bronze statuette was perhaps the most revealing of all Renaissance revivals. In this period collectors became so addicted to antique sculpture that they wished to have pieces literally to hand, pieces which they might fondle in their studies. On the whole they preferred nudes. At this time, however, Roman bronzes were hard to find and the few that had been dug up lacked the perfect finish demanded by the Renaissance connoisseur. So sculptors not unwillingly supplied the need in countless little figures of gods and mythological beings, derived from classical statues and modelled with exquisite refinement.
> HONOUR

We come back to the portego. On the wall to the right is a collection of c16 bronze panels, and in the room entered by the doorway on the far left a number of delightful, if minor, Florentine paintings. At the end of the portego away from the Canal, we find a recess with carved and gilded c15 ceiling and
Mantegna: *Saint Sebastian*
On a scroll painted at the foot of the picture you can read the words: 'nil nisi divinum stabile est caetera fumus'.

Take the small staircase up to the next floor.
On the far left wall
Francesco Guardi (attr.): *View of Piazzetta* and *View of Waterfront and Santa Maria della Salute*
The frescoes in the portego are more of historical than of artistic interest: the damp climate of Venice ensures a short life for painting in this medium. In the rooms entered at the loggia end of the portego are

some further paintings. Through the doorway on the right are some
delightful Flemish paintings and in the room on the left we may note
especially
Paris Bordone: *Venus Asleep with Cupid, in Landscape*
Van Dyck: *Portrait in Black*
Titian: *Venus*, in a c16 frame (believed to be a copy of his *Venus at the
Mirror* in the Hermitage)

Pass into the next room, take the stairs (with characteristic balustrade)
down to the floor below and leave through the entrance hall.

The vaporetto stop is at the end of the calle. The wait for the vaporetto
is the opportunity to see the buildings on the other side of the Canal – in
particular the fine c18 Palazzo Corner della Regina: you will see this a
little to the right, just beyond the Rio San Cassiano (the first side canal),
and beside a traghetto station.

From the vaporetto, we can look back at the Gothic façade of the
Ca'd'Oro. The open arcade at water level seems to derive from (and may
incorporate parts of) the earlier, Veneto-Byzantine, building on this site
– compare the Ca'da Mosto (p.172). The tracery of the Ducal Palace has
plainly influenced that of the *piano nobile* (first floor) here. The 'double
cable' moulding of the corners is especially fine.

> . . ., every Gothic palace has the appearance of enclosing as many rooms, and
> attaining as much strength, as is possible, with a minimum quantity of brick and
> stone. The traceries of the windows, which in Northern Gothic only support the
> *glass*, at Venice support the *building*; and thus the greater ponderousness of the
> *traceries* is only an indication of the greater lightness of the *structure*.
>   . . . And so in all the other palaces built at the time, consummate strength was
> joined with a lightness of form and sparingness of material, which rendered it
> eminently desirable that the eye should be convinced, by every possible
> expedient, of the stability of the building; and these twisted pillars at the angles
> are not among the least important means adopted for this purpose, for they seem
> to bind the walls together as a cable binds a chest.
> RUSKIN

> Ca'd'Oro represents the last flowering of the Venetian Gothic, and it is interesting
> to reflect that the Palazzo Medici Riccardi and Palazzo Pitti were being designed
> in Florence just about the time of its completion. The palace derives its name
> from the fact that Jean Charlier – 'Zuane di Francia', a French painter –
> gilded the friezes, cornices and ornamental merlons in 1431.
> MASSON

> During the whole of the fifteenth century, Venice was engaged in conquering
> neighbouring towns, over which Venetian nobles were appointed as governors.
> The Republican government of Venice gave special care to the regulations for

the development of trade, both in home and overseas markets. Her prosperity was due to a State commercial system, and was not the result of mere accident or of the enterprise of individuals. This successful trading community produced many kings of commerce, whose rivalry in display led to the erection of numerous fine palaces on the Grand Canal, which from their situation on the broad waterfront needed less protection against civic turmoil than was necessary in Florence and other inland cities, and so could be more splendid and open externally.

. . . the extreme heat of summer was here tempered by sea breezes, and to enjoy them, belvederes and balconies were usual, these all the more necessary in that the restricted island sites gave little room for gardens. On the other hand, the northern latitude and the winds that swept down from the snow-topped mountains, made fire-places almost essential, and the funnel-topped chimneys are a distinctive Venetian feature.

BANISTER FLETCHER

Frequently the balconies are not coeval with the houses, having been added or replaced at a later date. Very broadly, one can date Venetian balconies (though not the buildings behind) to within a hundred years or so by the form of the balustrade. The typical Quattrocento baluster was a slender classical colonette, while the stone hand rails often had seated lions or small stone busts at the corners. In the sixteenth century Sansovino introduced a new type of baluster borrowed from Michelangelo in Florence, which became extremely popular. This was broadest in the middle, with a cubic block at the centre. Sanmicheli at the same period also used balusters which were broader in the middle, but with a 'waist' at the centre. In the seventeenth century a more Baroque type of baluster, broader at the bottom, was adopted, sometimes alternating with uprights broader at the top. . . . The eighteenth century's Rococo taste favoured little curved balconies with wrought-iron railings.

HOWARD

Gobbo:

Master, young gentlemen, I pray you, which is the way to master Jew's?

Launcelot:

Turn up on your right hand, at the next turning, but at the very next turning of all, on your left; marry, at the very next turning, turn of no hand, but turn down indirectly to the Jew's house.

Gobbo:

By God's sonties, 'twill be a hard way to hit.

THE MERCHANT OF VENICE

Walk 7

San Marcuola – Ghetto – San Alvise – Madonna dell'Orto – San Stae

San Marcuola

Take the vaporetto to San Marcuola: well-head (1713) in campo, unfinished façade of church behind. The saint's name is perhaps a corruption of Hermagora, the Patriarch of Aquilea in the c8. A calle to the right of the church leads to the Rio terrà drio la Chiesa; turn left here, and when you can go no further, turn right (at the Calle de la Colona) then left along the broad street (Rio terrà San Leonardo), over the bridge (Ponte di Canareggio – illustrated on p.181) to the Campo San Geremia. On the left is the Palazzo Labia. This is now the regional headquarters of Italian radio and television (RAI), who have made an excellent job of restoring the first-floor room. Ask to see the magnificent Tiepolo frescoes.

On the walls
Tiepolo: *Banquet of Cleopatra* (above; *Time Carrying off Beauty*)
Tiepolo: *Embarkation of Cleopatra* (above: *Wind Blowing)*

On the ceiling
Tiepolo: *Poetry on a Winged Pegasus*

So far as I am concerned, Tiepolo painted largely in vain. I can admire the firm decision of his drawing and his skill in composition, but I can never lose the feeling that his right place is the wall of a restaurant or a theatre curtain. Still, since at the Palazzo Labia we find him decorating a banqueting hall with a secular subject, all is well.
LUCAS

There is no doubt that the famous supper scene, where Cleopatra is shown in the legendary act of dissolving a pearl in a goblet of vinegar, owes something of its inspiration to Veronese's *Supper in the House of Levi*, which is now in the Accademia, even in such small details as the dogs which appear in the right foreground of both compositions.
MASSON

To an earlier age even the subject might have seemed vulgar. But Tiepolo delights in its ostentation and its romantic qualities; there is nothing of high Roman terms in his treatment of it, and little that is specifically Egyptian either. Although the story derives from Pliny, this does not hinder Tiepolo from evolving out of the joint consul with Antony, Plancus, the bizarre oriental figure seated at the left of the table; and in the opposite fresco of *Antony and Cleopatra at the Harbour*, one of the flags gaily bears the German Eagle. The impression rather than exact fact is what matters; ostentation is suggested, not painted literally. The location of Egypt is conveyed by the obelisk and a pair of statues; the attendant soldiers are indicated simply by shafts of halberds rising into the sky; and down the long vista of the scene two lovers confront each other . . . . Whereas the *Banquet* had been the subject of a large picture before it became a fresco, the *Harbour Scene* was virtually Tiepolo's first and final large-scale treatment of the subject. The treatment of it seems rather freer, and possibly it was painted rather later than the *Banquet*. However fast Tiepolo worked, Mengozzi-Colonna (perhaps with assistance) had, on each wall, a considerable task to finish first; and there may well have been some interval for Tiepolo between the two chief scenes. The *Harbour Scene* is conceivably meant to show Cleopatra's landing after her triumphal progress up the river Cydnus, but Tiepolo does not bother to give very precise indications. The lovers advance – Cleopatra in patterned white brocade; their splendid cortege is suggested in small space by massed heads and one single noble horse; and behind them a gang-plank leads to the shell-like prow of a ship. Suggestions of a whole fleet are conveyed by purely theatrical means – brief glimpses of a mast and tackle and the huge sheet of a billowing sail.

The space of sky here seems really wet and windy. The façade frame of the fresco rises nearly to the ceiling, and there at its top astride the clouds the Winds themselves puff their cheeks to fill the sails. *The Banquet* is an immobile and tense scene; but the other wall is all movement, from the lovers who swing out towards the room to the flapping flags and prancing horses who emphasize the restless shifting pageant . . . .

Ignorant but imaginative, Tiepolo placed the scene firmly in sixteenth century Venice, where in fact for him all history took place . . . .

The greatest imaginative painter of the age was really outside the standards his age erected to judge painters. When Cochin said of one of Tiepolo's ceilings that it was 'more beautiful than natural' he indicated, as he thought, its failing. And against this canon of 'Nature' the great artists of the eighteenth century were often to seem culpable and even ridiculous. In England Gainsborough's portraits were to be called 'daubs'; in France Voltaire sneered at Watteau's work and Diderot said he would give *ten* Watteau's for a single Teniers. Tiepolo was, then, exercising his imagination in a chilly climate of critical appraisal. He might be popular with his compatriots, with aristocratic patrons in *retardier* countries; but two of his chief pictorial sources – religion and mythology – were themselves going out of favour. An age of scrutiny, as the eighteenth century supremely was, could hardly be expected to take Tiepolo's work seriously, and the more imaginative he was the more he invited criticism.
LEVEY

We leave the campo at the far right corner, along the Salizzada San Geremia (della Pescaria). After the bridge, left along the Fondamenta de

Canareggio. From here you can see the late c17 three-arched bridge (Ponte dei Tre Archi) – illustrated on pp.181 and 183.

Ghetto

Just after the vaporetto stop, there is an archway on the right – the Sotoportego del Ghetto. This will lead you to the Ghetto Vecchio and the Campo de le Scuole. Facing you is the Levantine synagogue, recently restored by Save Venice Inc. Very fine carved ceiling and pulpit by Brustolon. Opposite is the Spanish or Sephardic synagogue: much of the interior details is by Longhena; it is greatly in need of restoration. Out of the campiello, the Ponte de Gheto Vecio leads into the Ghetto Nuovo.

> At the far end of the campo (beside No.2921) is the Ponte di Ghetto Nuovo, one of the last iron bridges erected by the Austrians, which shows the splendid wrought-iron-work railings which were such an attractive contribution to the Venetian urban scene.
> HOWARD.

On the right-hand part of the range on the other side of the campo is the Jewish museum: the Curator shows the synagogues.

Jews in Venice were segregated, heavily taxed and subjected to a variety of restrictions. After 1516 they had to live on this island, their houses facing inwards, and the gates locked at night. But, unusually for a Christian state, they enjoyed the protection of the law. As Shakespeare's Merchant of Venice says,

> 'The duke cannot deny the course of law;
> For the commodity that strangers have
> With us in Venice if it be denied,
> Will much impeach the justice of this state;
> Since that the trade and profit of this city
> Consisteth of all nations.'

The community prospered, Italian and German Jews in the New Ghetto, and, later, Levantine Jews in the Old Ghetto. In 1635, the Spanish synagogue was rebuilt by Longhena. But the taxes outran the profit, and in 1735 the community was officially declared bankrupt.[1]

---

[1] Those with a particular interest in the Ghetto should arm themselves with the excellent *Jewish Art Treasures in Venice* published by International Fund for Monuments Inc. and available at their information centre at San Giovanni Evangelista (see p.148).

San Alvise

We leave the Ghetto under the Sotoportego del Ghetto Nuovo (beside No.2908). Go over the bridge, then left under the archway (Calle del Ghetto Novissimo), right at the end, under a rectangular arch, immediately left along the Calle dei Ormesini, over the bridge and straight into the Calle de la Malvasia, and over another bridge and straight along the Calle del Capitelo to the church of San Alvise. The façade is late c14 Gothic; the interior is a product of c16 re-arrangement and restoration.

On the left on entering and under the singing gallery are eight c15 panels of some charm (wrongly attributed to Carpaccio by Ruskin). Looking diagonally across the church we can see three works of Tiepolo. The earliest (1738–40) are on the right wall of the church, just before it narrows to the chancel.

Tiepolo: *The Flagellation* and *The Crowning with Thorns*

On the right wall immediately in the chancel
The Road to Calvary

The picture has an hysterical intensity which becomes displeasing, and the scene is too effective to be moving. Tiepolo was almost certainly sincere. But he was not the realist which he tried to be here, with many backward glances not only at sixteenth century Venetian art but also at Rembrandt. The healthy, cheerful people, dignified, well-dressed, of his usual imagining are pageant-people: what he has produced at S. Alvise are wax-works from the chamber of horrors. The spectacle is degrading, and the trumpets and horses and Roman eagles make a distasteful carnival of the road to Calvary. The three pictures are Tiepolo's most elaborate Passion compositions, and their religious grand-guignol atmosphere makes clear his unsuitability to deal with violent and horrific themes, whatever their source.
LEVEY

Tiepolo's energy, his feeling for splendour, his mastery over his craft, place him almost on a level with the great Venetians of the sixteenth century, although he never allows one to forget what he owes to them, particularly to Veronese. The grand scenes he paints differ from those of his predecessor not so much in mere inferiority of workmanship as in a lack of that simplicity and candour which never failed Paolo, no matter how proud the event he might be portraying. Tiepolo's people are haughty, as if they felt that to keep a firm hold on their dignity they could not for a moment relax their faces and figures from a monumental look and bearing. They evidently feel themselves so superior that they are not pleasant to live with, although they carry themselves so well, and are dressed with such splendour, that once in a while it is a great pleasure to look at them. It was Tiepolo's vision of the world that was at fault, and his

Veduta di Canal-Regio al Ponte dei tre Archi.

Veduta di Canal-Regio al Ponte di S. Geremia.

The Tre Archi Bridge over the canal of Canareggio was restored after the print on p.183 and has been slightly remodelled since. The bridge of San Geremia crosses the same canal near the Palazzo Labia. This pair of engraving was done by Antonio Pietro Zucchi (1726–95).

vision of the world was at fault only because the world itself was at fault. Paolo saw a world touched only by the fashions of the Spanish Court, while Tiepolo lived among people whose very hearts had been vitiated by its measureless haughtiness.
BERENSON

Return over the bridge and along the Calle del Capitelo, and turn left along the fondamenta (the Fondamenta della Sensa). After a while the Gothic façade of the church of the Madonna dell'Orto appears at the end of a waterway on the left. This is the Ponte Brazzo.

The next turning to the left is the Campo dei Mori. At the opposite corner, facing the water is one of the dilapidated late c13 statues, standing on Roman fragments: this one is popularly called 'Signor Antonio Rioba', a well-known figure in Venetian legend, whose name was used by authors of satires and lampoons.

Madonna dell'Orto

The other end of the campo leads to the church (restored, Italian Art and Archives Rescue Fund). It was Tintoretto's parish church and contains some of his finest works.

The building is an outstanding example of a c14 Gothic church. The early c15 façade effortlessly mixes with the Gothic elements of the Romanesque (the niches and blind arcading beneath the roof) and the Renaissance (the doorway).

First altar on right
Cima da Conegliano: *St John the Baptist and Saints*

(Above) The façade of the church of the Madonna dell'Orto (of the garden) is the most intact example of Venetian C15 architecture remaining today. The simple C16 Scuola on the left is attributed to Palladio. The district is poor and neglected, its fine palaces divided into miserable tenements (from the 'Gran Teatro di Venezia', but reproduced from an earlier source, c.1700).

(Below) The Tre Archi Bridge, built in 1688 by Andrea Tirali (1660–1737). Like so many similar structures it originally had no walls or balusters (from the 'Gran Teatro di Venezia').

On the right side of the nave, just past the fourth altar, we come to the door into the chapel, over which is
Tintoretto: *Presentation of the Virgin at the Temple*
Two large early works are on the side walls of the chancel: *Worship of the Golden Calf, with Moses Receiving the Tablets of the Law* and *Last Judgment*

On either side of the altar
Right side
Tintoretto: *Beheading of Saint Paul*
Left side
Tintoretto: *Apparition of the Cross to Saint Peter*

Returning along the N wall of the church we come to a side chapel (marble portraits on the walls), on the altar of which is
Tintoretto: *Saint Agnes Reviving the Roman*

The last side chapel we reach contains
Giovanni Bellini: *Madonna and Child*
(restored, IFM)

On the left outside the church is the c15 cloister, restored by its owner.
   Back through the Campo dei Mori, over the bridge, through the Calle Larga, and left at the fondamenta. This is the Fondamenta della Misericordia. There are places for coffee.
   Continuing along the Fondamenta della Misericordia, we take the first bridge to the Campo San Marziale, and its c17 church.

In the vault of the chancel
Ricci: *Holy Father and Angels*

On the ceiling of the church
Ricci: *Glory of Saint Martial* (centre)
Ricci: *Arrival of the Image of the Virgin,* and *The Image of the Virgin Carved on a Tree Trunk* (sides)

He is a disconcerting phenomenon since he began so much, while yet as an artist remaining insipid and usually uninspired. His very attachment to Veronese leads to comparisons in which he emerges eternally the loser. And the existence of Tiepolo, who learnt so much from him, leads to another comparison in which Ricci is defeated again.
   But as early as 1705 Ricci was capable of creating the luminous decorative effect of his ceiling in S. Marziale at Venice: an effect considerably enhanced by

recent cleaning. To come on this ceiling unexpectedly is to experience something of the excitement it must have generated when it was first shown. It is full of gaily-coloured airborne figures, as in the roundel of the *Arrival of the Virgin's statue*, and has something of the pastel effect of fresco although all the decoration is actually on canvas. Ricci at this time had not settled in Venice, but was still wandering about Italy and the rest of Europe. He had not become quite so obsessed with Veronese as he was to be later, and the S. Marziale ceiling is an unusual example of him creating something for himself, though not without hints from Correggio.
LEVEY

Out of the campo over the bridge, down the Calle Zancani, over the next bridge into Campo Santa Fosca. At the other end, a pink palazzo with an overhanging roof is the Palazzo Correr (c15 with c18 modifications); to the left a broad street leads – over a bridge – to a small campo. On the left is the church of San Felice: take the Calle del Tragheto opposite to the traghetto station.

If you look across the Canal you will see on the opposite bank, a little on the right, a large imposing c17 palazzo – the Palazzo Pesaro, the last work of Longhena (top storey completed later), and, just to the left of the opposite ferry station, the c18 Palazzo Corner della Regina.

Cross the Canal by traghetto. Look back to the right; just before the vaporetto station is the Ca' d'Oro (see p.173); looking to the left you can see examples of Venetian palazzo architecture of different periods: first an c18 palazzo (the lowest of the group), then an early c16 palazzo, with a finely proportioned Renaissance façade, then a façade of similar size, in c15 pointed-arch style (some later alterations), then a yellow-coloured building – an early c18 palazzo, and then – after the garden – the fine early c16 palazzo designed by Codussi – the Palazzo Vendramin Calergi. Wagner stayed here and died here in 1883.

Take the calle from the traghetto stop: the third opening on the right (Calle del Ravano) leads over two bridges and comes to a stop at a private bridge. Turn right here and cross the iron bridge at the end.

San Stae

At the head of the Campo San Stae is the late Baroque façade of the church of San Stae (San Eustachio).

Inside, there are several pictures on the walls of the chancel.
On the left wall, bottom row, right
Piazzetta: *St James Led to Martyrdom*

His *St. James Led to Martyrdom*, painted for St. Stae at Venice in 1717, make the work there of the rest of his contemporaries look very slight and artificial – except for that of the young Tiepolo[1] who was then briskly and misguidedly aping Piazzetta's style. It is true that Piazzetta's drama tends here to Melodrama; but it is significant that he has taken a scene lacking in all supernatural incident, and what he shows in fact is a vigorous old man dragged along in a contorted and confused way by a brawny, tawny, younger man. In character there seems nothing to choose between saint and executioner. Whereas the rococo, however defined, is always aiming to elevate the subject to an exciting operatic movement of grand gestures and radiant personalities, Piazzetta recalls the uncouth literalness of Loth, for example, and seems almost to 'debunk' his subject. Sebastian Ricci's *St. Peter Released*[2] from the same St. Stae series, was probably painted a very few years indeed after Piazzetta's picture there, but has obviously nothing in common with it . . . .
LEVEY

From here you can get back by vaporetto to San Marco and the Piazza.

---

[1] Right wall, bottom row right.　　[2] Left wall, bottom row middle.

Excursions

1 Lido

It is true that the beach is ugly and expensive and it is also true that virtually nothing remains of the sandy wilderness known to Goethe and Byron; nevertheless, if you are fond of sea-bathing and sun-bathing, go; the sand and the water are pleasant and clean, the bathing facilities are well organized, and the sail across the Lagoon (especially the return journey) is delightful.

I like to take the large boat from the Riva degli Schiavoni: it is quick; in the height of the season the sailings are fairly frequent; and the bar is efficient and cheap. Once on the Lido island, it is possible to eat on the way to the beach or on the beach; if you are taking picnic food, do not take fruit – you can buy this from stalls near the beach. (Try the pieces of coconut arranged in tiers under little fountains.)

The municipal beach is on the left, when you come to the sea. (Farther to the left – and a long way away – there is a free beach.) To the right are the beaches run by the big hotels; use of the cabins there is reserved to guests of those hotels, but the bars and restaurants are open to the public. Beyond these is a public beach, with a pleasant restaurant and bar – a good place for a picnic.

2 Burano–Torcello

The boat for Torcello leaves from the Fondamenta Nuove. This is not as far as it looks: from the Piazza, under the Clock Tower, right at the Ramo San Zulian, round behind the church, straight on over two bridges to Campo Santa Maria Formosa, out of the far side (by the clock) down the Calle Larga, fourth calle on the left to San Zanipolo, and follow the Canal beside the hospital to the Fondamenta Nuove.

Alternatively one may take the vaporetto line 5 (circolare sinistra) from the Riva degli Schiavoni as far as Murano and get the Torcello boat at Murano Faro.

In the Lagoon we see the cemetery island, San Michele.

As we go by the Cemetery of S. Michele, Piero the gondolier and Giovanni improve us with a little solemn pleasantry. 'It is a small place', says Piero, 'but there is room enough for all Venice in it'. 'It is true', assents Giovanni, 'and here we poor folks become land-owners at last'.
HOWELLS

. . . but the dead are only allowed to rest for ten years; then, unless an annual fee is paid, the bones are taken up and thrown, without distinction, into a vast common pit at the end of the island.
HARE

The boat stops close to the façade of Codussi's church of San Michele in Isola.

Codussi effectively exploited the contrast between the white façade and the dark openings of the doorway and windows. These shapes were kept very simple, and the four strong contrasting areas are important elements of the design. Smaller dots of contrast appear in the upper areas; four porphyry and *verde antico* roundels frame the oculus while a fifth accent, an ellipse, is centred in the semicircular tympanum. Not all of the colour contrasts are strong, however; the cornices of the quadrant arches flanking the central field of the second storey, the central field itself and the semicircular pediment above it are edged with subtle, light blue-grey marble.
    Codussi was extremely sensitive to texture, and the most remarkable aspect of the façade is the variety of textures kept in balance: the stone pattern of the lower storey, the shells in the quadrants, the veined marble around the oculus, the radial flutes of the corona of the tympanum. Even the Albertian frieze inscriptions, in handsome and correct ancient Roman lettering, the first of this type to be found in Venice, make a texture across what would otherwise be plain surfaces.
LIEBERMAN

The next stop is Murano. The Venetian glass industry was established here, and not in the city itself, because of the fire hazard. In the c16 the finest glass in the world was made here and Murano enjoyed a virtual monopoly in the manufacture of mirrors, but little of its present-day production is of any interest. The island does have however two churches of great interest – the c16 church of San Pietro Martire, with one of the most luminous of Giovanni Bellini's paintings – the *Barbarigo Madonna* – in the right aisle; and the c12 church of San Donato, to visit which is in itself sufficient reason to stop at Murano. The exterior of the beautiful Romanesque apse is seen from the campo (good stop for coffee). The interior of the apse retains the original c12 mosaic – *Virgin Praying* – in the cove; the recently restored floor (restored, VIP) is of marble and coloured glass, also c12.

The boat now crosses the Lagoon to Mazzorbo. In front and to the right are the islands of Sant'Erasmo and Le Vignole.

> A most pleasant sunset hour can be spent on the Lagoon, by taking the
> *Sant'Erasmo* waterbus any late afternoon from Fondamenta Nuove . . . . The
> church at *Sant'Erasmo* is well worth a visit, being originally a romanesque
> building: the fine font is Byzantine. There is a good cafe. The return journey
> during sunset is one of the finest Lagoon experiences one can have. The people on
> *Vignole* and on *Sant'Erasmo* are welcoming, very hard-working, and ill paid by
> the middlemen who fetch the vegetables and fruit they grow for Venice Markets.
> SPRIGGE

Before the boat enters the Canal of Mazzorbo, we can see on the right the cypresses of San Francesco del Deserto.

> This lonely islet-monastery can be visited directly from Riva Schiavoni or from
> the Lido on another Torcello waterbus . . . which calls at San Francesco. But in
> high summer that would be a visit in a crowd. Best of all is a gondola or a sandolo
> (two oars) from Mazzorbo or Burano, a very pleasant cross-water journey. There
> is a peacock on the island.
> SPRIGGE

We stop at Mazzorbo – a quiet spot, with a c14 church, and vineyards. It is connected to Burano by a wooden bridge.

The next stop is Burano. This picturesque, but very spick and span, fishing village has a restaurant with character ('Da Romano') and an early Tiepolo *Crucifixion* in the oratory of Santa Barbara, near the church.

The next stop is Torcello. The island is now sparsely populated and makes a refreshing change from the crowded and intensely urban atmosphere of Venice, but it has one expensive and two modest restaurants and the path behind the basilica leads to some good picnic spots.

> The inlet which runs nearest to the base of the campanile is not that by which
> Torcello is commonly approached. Another, somewhat broader and overhung
> alder copse, winds out of the main channel of the lagoon up to the very edge of
> the little meadow which was once the plaza of the city, and there, stayed by a

---

(Overleaf) Islands and Chioggia, a C18 plate most likely by Antonio Pietro Zucchi.

Isola di Murano presso a Venezia.

Isola di S. Michele di Murano presso a Venezia.

Isola di S. Giorgio Maggiore di Venezia.

Città di Chioggia nel Dogado Veneto.

few grey stones which present some semblance of a quay, forms its boundary at one extremity. Hardly larger than an English farmyard, and roughly enclosed on each side by broken palings and hedges of honeysuckle and briar the narrow field retires from the water's edge, traversed by a scarcely traceable footpath, for some forty or fifty paces, and then expanding into the form of a small square, with buildings on three sides of it, the fourth being that which opens to the water. Two of these, that on our left, and that in front of us as we approach from the canal, are so small that they might well be taken for out-houses of the farm, though the first is a conventual building, and the other aspires to the title of the 'Palazzo Pubblico', both dating as far back as the beginning of the fourteenth century; the third, the octagonal church of Santa Fosca, is far more ancient than either, yet hardly on a larger scale. Though the pillars of the portico which surrounds it are of pure Greek marble, and their capitals are enriched with delicate sculpture, they, and the arches they sustain, together only raise the roof to the height of a cattle-shed; and the first strong impression which the spectator receives from the whole scene is that whatever sin it may have been which has on this spot been visited with so utter a desolation, it could not at least have been ambition. Nor will this impression be diminished as we approach or enter the larger church, to which the whole group of building is subordinate. It has evidently been built by men in flight and distress, who sought in the hurried erection of their island church such a shelter for their earnest and sorrowful worship as, on the one hand, would not attract the eyes of their enemies by its splendour and yet, on the other, might not awaken too bitter feelings by its contrast with the churches which they had seen destroyed. There is visible everywhere a simple and tender effort to recover some of the form of the temples which they had loved, and to do honour to God by that which they were erecting, while distress and humiliation prevented the desire, and prudence precluded the admission, either of luxury of ornament or magnificence of plan. The exterior is absolutely devoid of decoration, with the exception only of the western entrance and the lateral door, of which the former has carved side-posts and architrave, and the latter crosses of rich sculpture; while the mossy stone shutters of the windows, turning on huge rings of stone, which answer the double purpose of stanchions and brackets, cause the whole building rather to resemble a refuge from Alpine storm than the cathedral of a populous city; and internally, the two solemn mosaics of the eastern and western extremities – one representing the Last Judgment, the other the Madonna, her tears falling as her hands are raised to bless – and the noble range of pillars which enclose the space between, terminated by the high throne for the pastor and the semicircular raised seats for the superior clergy, are expressive at once of the deep sorrow and the sacred courage of men who had no home left them upon earth, but who looked for one to come, of men 'persecuted, but not foresaken, cast down but not destroyed'.

RUSKIN

The town was built by refugees from the barbarian invasions of Roman Italy. Later, the centre of economic life moved to the Rialto, and the settlements in this part of the Lagoon decayed.

At the end of the water-way, we reach the church of Santa Fosca, c11–c12, but much restored.

> It is a Greek cross martyrion with truncated arms and a large dome on squinches. The dome was never completed and it has been argued, significantly perhaps for understanding Venice's role as bridge between east and west, that the Greek workmen who began the church deserted the job, leaving behind only local masons who were not competent to construct the dome . . .
> LAURITZEN

The Cathedral, beyond (restored, International Torcello Committee) is mainly c11. Down the sides of the main door, c9 interwoven designs and crosses, c11 grape-vine design. Very fine mosaics decorate the interior. In the apse, twelve apostles (c12 but much restored) in Ravenna style; Virgin, c13; on opposite wall, c12–c15 *Universal Judgment* (upper parts heavily restored in c19); more in chapel to right of main altar.

In the apse of the chapel to the right of the main altar are c12–c13 mosaics depicting Jesus with Archangels Gabriel and Michael; saints below. The arch preceding it is decorated with a c11 or c12 copy of the c6 ceiling of the chancel in San Vitale, Ravenna – with angels supporting a central medallion, the ground being filled with green and gold scrolls. The capitals are particularly attractive: they are mostly c11, but the second and third on the N side of the nave are c6.

Beside the main door, a font, supported on a piece of column.

> This history of Torcello has for its background in the 4th and 5th Centuries the savagery and slaughter of the Migration period. Like a late reminder of this a font of barbarian vigour stands on a column, half-forgotten, in the gloomiest corner of the church. Here we have a Lombard or Friuli craftsman and for once can sense the under-tone of non-classical violence over which the order of Mediterranean culture only triumphed after heavy fighting.
> DECKER

The rood screen is made up of c15 painted panels supported on columns, with early c11 Byzantine marble panels beneath. Fragments of other panels make up the stair to the pulpit, admired by Ruskin.

In the S chapel, on the floor, is an early c14 tomb.

> If one follows the path running along the far side of the basilica, hopping up and down banks and across little wastes covered with flowers, grape hyacinths, poppies, violets and sweet wild asparagus with the off-shore barene blue with

sea-lavender in the autumn and speckled with white foraging seagulls, one will arrive at the outlying farmhouse of San Antonio where one can look back on the apse of the basilica and the cheerful waterfront of Burano.
GUITON

3 Gesuiti Church and Oratorio dei Crociferi

(by gondola)

If you can afford a gondola ride, on no account miss it. Possible rides are endless; the only rule is to agree the duration and price with the gondolier before you start. A tariff is displayed on the boat.

The gondola is a complicated craft, which has developed over the centuries (recall the early version in the *St Ursula* series – p.91) and reached its present form at the end of the last century. One curious feature among many (see T. Holme: *Gondola, Gondolier*) is the inbuilt list, which rights itself under the weight of the gondolier. It was devised as a mode of transport; to experience it in the most authentic fashion, the journey should have an aim. Here I propose an excursion to a showy and extravagant example of c18 Baroque – the church of the Gesuiti. Ask the gondolier to wait beside the campo.

Travellers may often complain of the weariness of the Venetian sights, and of their being too much like one another. It is quite true that they are so, but let those who are bored sit still in their gondolas.
HARE

The Gesuiti can alternatively be reached from the Fondamenta Nuove: from the vaporetto stop (line 5, circolare sinistra; or on foot as described for Walk 2), take the bridge over the Rio dei Gesuiti and the next turning on the left.

The collapse of the east end of this church was averted by timely action by Save Venice Inc. Notice the fine ceiling frescoes, the marble 'carpet' on steps of high altar.

On the altar on the N side, nearest to the entrance
Titian: *Martyrdom of Saint Lawrence*
(light switch by column on right). The figure of the saint is modelled on a Hellenistic statue, the Dying Gaul, now in the Archeological Museum (p.199).

Santa Fosca.

Titian's art underwent somewhat of a change about 1540. The problems posed by mannerism are reflected in his work and shake his serene vision of the world. He wrenches his forms, foreshortens his figures and underscores his lighting by a dramatic use of chiaroscuro, particularly in the *Martyrdom of Saint Lawrence* (1557). There are relatively few important Titians remaining in Venice.
CHASTEL

In this virtuoso night piece, the beam from heaven, the torches and the glowing fire beneath St. Lawrence's grille, illuminate the pagan idol, flicker on the marble temple and glint on the soldiers' helmets. One is even inclined to suspect that the painting is an excuse for the pyrotechnic effects and the use of dark, rich colour rather than an attempt to render the Saint's agony. Apart from a fresco by Raphael in the Vatican, it is the first successful nocturne in the history of art. Like the *Assumption* in the Frari, it anticipates the baroque style. It therefore exerted considerable influence when night-pieces became so popular throughout Europe in the seventeenth century.
HONOUR

Altar in N transept
Tintoretto: *Assumption*

In the Sacristy (entrance to the right of the *Assumption*) all the paintings (except the four evangelists over the door) are by Palma il Giovane.

Opposite the church is the Oratorio dei Crociferi (open mornings) recently restored by its present owners, I R E; a booklet is available. All the paintings inside are by Palma il Giovane, except that on the high altar, which is by a c17 Dutch painter, Pietro de Coster.

The Campo dei Gesuiti as seen in the 'Gran Teatro di Venezia' shows the Jesuit church at the far end of the square on the right before it was completed.

The finished façade of the Gesuiti church can be seen in Vissentini's engraving of Canaletto's drawing published in 1754.

Appendices

1 Table of Events

c5–c7	Barbarian invasions of Roman Empire. Torcello and other islands settled by refugees from mainland.
697	First Doge.
811–27	Seat of government moved to Rialto (Rivo Alto).
829	Remains of Saint Mark brought from Alexandria (p.22).
c9–c11	Growth of sea trade and naval power.
1044	San Marco consecrated.
1177	Pope Alexander III and Emperor Frederick Barbarossa reconciled (p.36).
1204	Armies of IVth Crusade take Constantinople: Venice acquires large territories in Near East and immense quantities of plunder.
c13–c14	Long struggle with Genoa, rival maritime power; Venetian victory at Chioggia 1380.
1310	Unsuccessful rebellion of Bajamonte Tiepolo (p.113).
1355	Unsuccessful bid for power by Doge Marin Faliero (p.52).
1453	Constantinople falls to Turks.
Late c15	Loss of several eastern colonies to Turks; defeat of navy at Sapienza (1441) beginning of three centuries of gradual decline.
1498	Vasco da Gama sails round Africa.
c16	Austrian-Spanish Hapsburgs expand on mainland, Turks in east. Loss of Morea (Peleponnese) and Cyprus (fate of Marcantonio Bragadin – p.122).
1606	Climax of long quarrel with Rome, Venice excommunicated.
c17	Continued struggle with Turks. Loss of Crete. Short-lived reconquest of Peleponnese.
c18	Foreign defeats, shrinking trade, social atrophy; carnivals and masquerades.
1797	Surrender to Napoleon, who passed town to Austria.
1805	Ten years under Napoleonic French rule.
1815–68	Austrian colony; era of particular oppression and poverty.
1868	Joined to Italy.

2 Special Interests

(i) MUSEUMS, GALLERIES AND PERMANENT EXHIBITIONS

1	Accademia (p.74)	Pictures
2	Scuola di San Giorgio (p.106)	Pictures by Carpaccio
3	Greek Institute (p.108)	Icons
4	Ca'd'Oro (p.173)	Furniture, Persian carpets
5	Palazzo Rezzonico (p.155)	c18 pictures and furnishings
6	Sansovino Library (p.43)	Bindings – Byzantine, Venetian and foreign, c10–c18 Codexes – Byzantine, Venetian and Italian
7	Zecca (Marciana Library) (p.44)	Codexes (Greek and Latin). Books, manuscripts, incunabulae
8	San Marco Treasury (p.39)	Byzantine goldsmiths' work, icons, bindings, Byzantine and Oriental objects (mainly ecclesiastical)
9	San Marco: Marciano Museum (above narthex of Basilica)	Flemish tapestries, Persian carpets
10	Doge's Palace (p.48)	Armoury
11	Arsenal (p.103)	Naval museum
12	Casa Goldoni (see under 'Courtyards')	Theatrical library
13	Scuola di San Giovanni Evangelista (p.148)	Architectural fragments, sculpture
15	Palazzo Querini-Stampalia (p.117)	Library, pictures, c18 and early c19 furniture
16	Archaeological Museum (the entrance is under the Sansovino Library)	
17	Patriarchal Seminary (next to Salute – p.64ff)	Pictures, sculpture, lapidary collection
18	Correr Museum (p.56ff)	Venetian Art and History collection, including (apart from the fine picture gallery) documents, robes, coins, seals, naval souvenirs and arms, and the Museum of the Risorgimento (illustrating the history of Venice from the fall of the Republic to 1945)
19	Fondaco dei Turchi (to San Marcuola vaporetto station, then across the canal by traghetto)	Natural History
20	Palazzo Venier dei Leoni (p.94)	Peggy Guggenheim Collection – c20 pictures
21	Palazzo Pisani (p.162)	Musical instruments
22	Murano Glass Museum (Murano – p.188)	Glass
23	Museum of Burano Lace (Burano – p.199)	Lace
24	Lagoon Museum (Torcello – p.187)	Fragments found at Torcello
25	Fortuny (Palazzo Fortuny) (Campo San Bendetto, 3780 San Marco), (off Calle de la Mandola – p.164)	Fortuny fabrics
26	Abbazia Nuova della Misericordia (not far from Madonna dell'Orto – p.182)	Sculpture and decorative stonework

27	Cini Museum (p.70)	Paintings
28	Sant' Apollonia (p.110)	Restored Paintings

(ii) COURTYARDS

1   No.6359. Calle della Testa (in front of Santi Giovanni e Paolo, p.120ff), take the Ponte del Cavallo; the Calle is on the right).
2   No.2793. Calle dei Nomboli – Casa Goldoni – (from the vaporetto station of San Tomà, take Calle del Tragheto until it opens out into a small square on the right. Through the square turn left along the Fondamenta San Tomà, and go over the Ponte San Tomà).
3   San Giorgio dei Greci – Churchyard with c15 well-head (109).
4   Ca'd'Oro (p.173ff).
5   Palazzo Contarini del Bovolo (p.164f).
6   Larger and more formal courtyards will be found in the Doge's Palace (p.48ff) and Palazzo Pisani (p.162).

(iii) CLOISTERS

1   Sant'Apollonia (p.110).
2   Carmini (p.151f).
3   Cypress Cloister and Bay Tree Cloister – Cini Foundation (p.70).
4   San Francesco della Vigna (p.107f).

(iv) GARDENS

1   Palazzo Venier dei Leoni (housing the Peggy Guggenheim Collection) (p.94f).
2   Eden Garden (Giudecca island: by boat to the Redentore, the garden lies along the nearby canal, the Ramo Campiello al Rio della Croce) — Laid out with flowers and lawns. Belongs to Princess Aspasia of Greece.
3   Patriarchal Seminary (vaporetto stop Salute)
4   Palazzo Grassi (vaporetto stop San Samuele) — c18 garden, now with open-air theatre
5   Cini Foundation, San Giorgio (p.70)

(v) THEATRES

An evening at the Fenice is imperative. The entrance halls were remodelled in 1957, but the interior, after being burnt in 1836, was remade as it was when it was first built in 1792 (p.161).

Other theatres are open intermittently, including an open-air theatre at the Palazzo Grassi. The Institute of Theatre Studies in the Casa Goldoni houses a library and memorials of the life and times of the c18 Venetian writer Goldoni.

(vi) VILLAS OF THE VENETO

The 'Malcontenta', the Villa Pisani at Stra and other villas can be visited by motor launch (apply CIT, Piazza San Marco). These and others can easily be reached by car. There are car-hire offices near the Piazzale Roma.

(vii) RESTORATION

The most interesting thing which has happened between the first and this
edition of this book is the restoration of the innumerable monuments, which has
been taken under the wing of the Italian Government and the Italian and other
voluntary organizations. I hope I have said enough in the text to impose on the
reader a conscious sense of indebtedness to these bodies. A number of outstanding
examples are mentioned in the course of the walks: those made before the 1966
flood – the Cini (p.70) and the Palazzo Labia (p.177); and those particularly
distinguished examples effected since the flood – the churches of the Pietà (p.103),
Santo Stefano (p.162), Zobenigo (p.162); the Loggetta (p.26); the Tintoretto
pictures in the Scuola San Rocco (p.137). Perhaps the most distinguished – the
true model for all restoration work of this kind – is the church of San Nicolò dei
Mendicoli (see optional excursion p.154).

Further information can be obtained from UNESCO, San Marco 63 (in the Palazzo
Reale in the Procuratie Nuove) and International Fund for Monuments, Venice
Committee, San Polo 2454 (San Giovanni Evangelista.).

3 Table of Artists

ELSEWHERE IN ITALY	VENICE	ELSEWHERE IN EUROPE
Giotto	Paolo Veneziano c.1290–1358	
Donatello	Jacopo Bellini 1400–1470	Van Eyck
Piero della Francesca	Antonio Vivarini c.1415–c.1484	
Mantegna	Gentile Bellini 1429–1507	Memling
Verrocchio	Giovanni Bellini 1430–1516	
	Bartolomeo Vivarini c.1432–c.1499	
	Codussi c.1440–1504	
Perugino	Alvise Vivarini c.1446–c.1505	
	Andrea da Murano?–1502	
Leonardo	Cima da Conegliano 1459–1518	
	Carpaccio c.1465–1525	Dürer
	Giorgione c.1478–1510	Holbein
	Palma the Elder 1480–1528	
Michelangelo	Lotto 1480–1556	
	Sansovino 1486–1570	
	Titian c.1488–1576	El Greco
	Basaiti c.1500–	
	Paris Bordone 1500–1571	
	Palladio 1508–1580	Rubens
	Tintoretto 1518–1594	
	Aless. Vittoria 1524–1608	
	Veronese 1530–1588	Van Dyck
	Palma the Younger 1544–1628	
A. Carraci	Longhena 1568–1662	
Giordano	Bombelli 1635–1716	Heinz
Claude	Amigoni 1675–1752	

Piazzetta 1682–1754	Watteau
G. B. Tiepolo 1696–1770	Hogarth
Canaletto 1697–1768	Wilson
Longhi 1702–1785	
Guardi 1712–1793	
Bellotto 1720–1780	
Giandomenico Tiepolo 1727–1804	
Canova 1757–1822	

4 Staying and Eating in Venice

Michelin is, as always, reliable on hotels. It is good on 'star' restaurants. 'Non-star' restaurants it can undervalue and overvalue: a simple rule in this class of restaurant is that the more difficult it is to find the better it is likely to be.

Anyone who wants a really cheap meal can go out to a bakery which has its own pizza oven and buy a large slice of pizza for a few lire, repair to the nearest bottigleria or wine shop, and there drink a litre of wine and eat his pizza for little more than a shilling . . .
ELIZABETH DAVID

Allowing for changes in money value, this is still true. You can easily and cheaply assemble a picnic lunch out of bread, cheeses, olives and ham, with fresh fruit and a bottle of wine. It is also possible to eat very well in Venice – at, of course, a very much higher price; this perhaps is the moment of stress that Italian cooking at its best is very much more distinguished than is commonly believed: it is seasonal and highly regional.

    Elizabeth David has collected some traditional Venetian recipes and gives other Venetian recipes based on chefs' recipes from restaurants in Venice. This is her list.

HORS D'ŒUVRE
Pasta in brodo	Pasta in broth
Crostin	Fried bread with cheese and anchovies
Vitello tonnato	Veal with tunny fish sauce

RISOTTO
Risotto in capro roman	Mutton risotto
Risotto de secole	Veal risotto
Risotto de scampi	Scampi risotto
Risotto di peoci	Mussel risotto

FISH
Zuppa di peoci	Cooked mussels
Grancevole	Crabs
Molecche	Soft shell crabs
Scampi alla griglia	Grilled scampi
Triglie all veneziana	Red mullet in wine
Sogiole all veneziana	Sole with wine sauce
Coda di rospo	Monkfish tail
Pesce San Pietro	John Dory
Baccalà montecato	Creamed salt cod

OTHER DISHES

Fegato alla veneziana	Fried liver and onion
Carciofi alla veneziana	Venetian artichokes
Filetto Casanova	Fillet steak with brandy and marsala
Polenta	Cooked maize
Aranci caramellizzati	Caramelized oranges

5 Glossary

Bacino	port
Calle	street
Campo	square, open space
Campiello	small square
Casa (Ca')	house
Corte, Cortile	courtyard
Fondamenta	street along a waterway
Ponte	bridge
Ramo	narrow street
Rio	waterway
Rio terrà	filled-in Rio
Riva	shore or bank, paved to form street
Salizzada	paved street
Sottoportico (Sotoportego)	covered passageway
Traghetto	rowboat ferry

Bibliography

Andrieux, M. *Daily Life in Venice in the time of Casanova*. Transl. by Mary Fitton. Allen & Unwin 1972.

Arslan, E. *Gothic Architecture in Venice*. Transl. by Anne Engel. Phaidon 1971.

Berenson, B. *The Italian Painters of the Renaissance*. Clarendon Press 1930.

Berenson B. *On Lotto*. Putnam 1895.

Berger, J. *Permanent Red*. Methuen 1960.

Brion, M. *Venice, The Masque of Italy*. Elek 1962.

Bull, G. *Venice, The Most Triumphant City*. Folio Society 1980.

Burckhardt, J. *The Civilisation of the Renaissance in Italy*. Transl. S. G. C. Middlemore. 3rd ed. Phaidon 1956.

Cessi, F. *Tiepolo: the life and work of the artist*. Transl. Pearl Sanders. Thames & Hudson 1971.

Chambers, D. S. *The Imperial Age of Venice*. Thames & Hudson 1970.

Chastel, A. 'Venice Observed' (notes on the plates). *L'Œil*.

Churchill, K. *Italy and English Literature 1764–1930*. Macmillan 1980.

David, E. *Italian Food*. Macdonald 1954, Penguin Books 1963.

Decker, H. *Venice*. Thames & Hudson 1957.

Demus, O. *A Renaissance of Early Christian Art in 13th Century Venice*. Late Classical and Mediaeval Studies in honour of Albert Matthias Friend Jr. edited by K. Weitzman. Princeton University Press 1955 (pp348–361).

Demus, O. *The Church of San Marco in Venice*. Dumbarton Oaks Research Library and Collection, Trustees for Harvard University 1960.

Demus, O. *The Mosaics of San Marco in Venice*. 4 vols. University of Chicago Press 1984.

Eeles, A. *Canaletto*. Hamlyn 1967.

Fay, S. and Knightley, P. *The Death of Venice*. André Deutsch 1976.

Fletcher, Sir Banister. *A History of Architecture on the Comparative Method*. 13th ed. Athlone Press 1975.

Goethe, J. W. von: *Italian Journey*. Transl. Rev. A. J. W. Morrison and Charles Nisbet,. Collins.

Gombrich, E. H. *The Story of Art*. 12th ed. Phaidon 1972.

Gould, C. *An Introduction to Italian Renaissance Painting*. Phaidon 1957.

Guiton, S. *No Magic Eden*. Hamish Hamilton 1972.

Guiton, S. *A World by Itself*. Hamish Hamilton 1977.

Hare, A. J. C. and St Clair Baddeley. *Venice*. 6th ed. Allen & Unwin 1904.

Holme, T. *Gondola, Gondolier*. Gentry Books 1971.

Honour, H. *The Companion guide to Venice*. Collins 1965, second ed. 1977.

Howard, D. *Jacopo Sansovino: Architecture and Patronage in Renaissance Venice*. Yale University Press 1975.

Howard, D. *The Architectural History of Venice*. Batsford 1980.

Lane, Frederick C. *Venice, A Maritime Republic*. John Hopkins 1973.

Lauritzen, P. *Venice: A Thousand*

Years of Culture and Civilization. Weidenfeld & Nicolson **1978**.

Lauritzen, P. and Zielcke, Z. *Palaces of Venice.* Phaidon **1978**.

Levey, M. *Painting in XVIII Century Venice.* Phaidon **1959**.

Lieberman, R. *Renaissance Architecture in Venice.* Muller **1982**.

Links, J. G. *Venice for Pleasure.* Bodley Head **1966**, revised ed. **1979**.

Lorenzetti, G. *Venice and its Lagoons.* Transl. J. Guthrie. Istituto Poligrafico dello Stato **1926**, English transl. **1961**, republished **1975**.

Lowe, A. *La Serenissima.* Cassell **1974**.

Lucas, E. V. *A Wanderer in Venice.* 8th ed. Methuen **1914**.

Lutyens, M. *Effie in Venice.* John Murray **1965**.

McAndrew, J. *Venetian Architecture of the Early Renaissance.* Cambridge, Mass. **1980**.

Masson, G. *Italian villas and palaces.* Thames & Hudson **1959**.

Morris, J. *Venice.* Faber & Faber **1960**, revised ed. **1983**.

Morris, J. *The Venetian Empire.* Faber & Faber **1980**.

Morris, J. (Ed.) John Ruskin: *The Stones of Venice.* Faber & Faber **1981**.

Murano, M. (with Mulas, V. transl. by Quigly, I.) *Invitation to Venice.* Paul Hamlyn **1963**.

Norwich, J. J. *Venice, the Rise to Empire.* Allen Lane **1977**.

Norwich, J. J. *The Greatness and the Fall.* Allen Lane **1981**.

Pevsner, N. *An Outline of European Architecture.* Penguin Books **1961**, new ed. Allen Lane **1973**.

Piatelli, A. A. (introduction). *Jewish Art Treasures in Venice.* International Fund for Monuments Inc. [n.d.].

Pignatti, T. *The Venice of Carpaccio.* Skira **1958**.

Pincus, D. *The Arco Foscari: The Building of a Triumphal Archway in Fifteenth Century Venice.* Garland, New York and London **1976**.

Robertson, G. *Giovanni Bellini.* Oxford University Press **1968**.

Rosand, David. *Painting in Cinquecento Venice.* Yale **1982**.

Rowdon, M. *The Fall of Venice.* Weidenfeld & Nicolson **1970**.

Ruskin, J. *The Stones of Venice.* **1853**, 4th ed. Allen & Unwin **1886**.

Ruskin, J. *Modern Painters.* 2nd ed. Allen & Unwin **1892** (see Morris, J.).

Rylands, Philip. *Introduction to Blue Guide to Venice.* (Ed. Macadam) Benn **1980**.

Shaw-Kennedy, R. *Art and architecture in Venice.* Sidgwick & Jackson **1972**.

Snowdon/Hart *A View of Venice.* Olivetti **1972**.

Sprigge, S. *The Lagoon of Venice.* Parrish **1961**.

Steer, J. *A concise history of Venetian painting.* Thames & Hudson **1970**.

Valieri, D. (with Duran, F. and Palluccini, R.) *Venise.* Librairie Hachette **1957**.

Wilde, J. *Venetian Art from Bellini to Titian.* Oxford University Press **1974**.

Wittkower, R. *Art and architecture in Italy.* 3rd rev. ed. Penguin Books **1973**.

Index